Teach

Stephen Higgins

Published by Stephen Higgins, 2024.

While every precaution has been taken in the preparation of this book, the publisher assumes no responsibility for errors or omissions, or for damages resulting from the use of the information contained herein.

TEACH

First edition. January 22, 2024.

Written by Stephen Higgins.

Table of Contents

Introduction 1

In The Classroom 5

Administration..50

Staff...87

Students 102

Interviews... 138

Afterword.. 169

For Kathy

Introduction

The first three years of Teaching
    Year 1 – Worrying about classroom control
    Year 2 – Worrying about content
    Year 3 – Worrying about office politics and administration
This was pointed out to me in my first few weeks of teaching, and I did not forget it. It is essentially true. Everyone worries about actually controlling that bunch of kids in front of them. Then, everyone worries that they are teaching the right stuff to that bunch of kids in front of them. And then, when they have pretty well settled into a life in teaching, all anyone worries about are the directives being fired at them by faceless administrators.

I would like to point out that this is not an academic text. This fact will become abundantly clear as you read through it, but I did want to point that fact out early. You will not find claims backed up with rigorous research and peer review. You will not read detailed discourse about the latest educational theories that have sprung from work done in Europe and transplanted to Australia. You also will not encounter a new educational program that will claim to improve Educational Outcomes in classrooms across Australia, with supporting software, lecture series and textbook. What I am presenting here will not be forced upon schools as a part of a new way of teaching. I mean, that would be nice for sales, but I am not expecting it.

Everything in this book is based on what I have experienced in my teaching career. Some of it is based on advice from my colleagues, and some is just common sense. I have taught, officially, for over 20 years. That is to say I was employed by the Education Department in Victoria, Australia to teach High School students between the ages of 12 to 18. I have also taught adults who wanted to learn how to write short stories, and I taught my wife how to drive. These three disciplines are not as far apart as you might think.

I have worked in a variety of fields. I have been a pen pusher in the public service. I have worked in plant nurseries. I have worked in the Department of Agriculture breeding peas. This sounds more esoteric than it was. It was a great job. One day I was in the laboratory, and the next I was out on the grey cracking plains of the Wimmera driving a tractor around. I have worked part time for Australia Post, sorting letters. I have continued to edit and co publish Aurealis, a digital Science Fiction and Fantasy magazine. I have pumped petrol, sold swimming pools, cut up chickens and I have recorded and sold music (Find it on Spotify!). And, with Michael Pryor, I co-host the podcast, Apocryphal Australia. As you can probably gather, I have had some life experience before I began teaching. Indeed I was in my mid-forties when I started my first full time job in teaching.

I also completed my degree and Diploma of Education late. I was studying part time by correspondence with Monash University for years. I didn't even know I would go into teaching until I had nearly completed my degree. I remember being envious of people who knew what they were going to do with their lives when they were still in High School. I had no idea. This sort of information and life experience is useful when talking to students about what they want to do after school. Many of them are convinced you have to know what you will do before you complete secondary education. They seem relieved to find out that they can decide later and indeed that you are allowed to change jobs later in life. This is probably just as well in my case. Teaching high school students has been the hardest and most rewarding job I have had. It has been tons of fun, and it has been gruelling. I guess most jobs have their highs and lows and I think teaching does too... It's just that its highs and lows are more extreme.

If you are reading this, you are either contemplating a career in teaching or you are actually already teaching, and you might be looking for a way to make it all easier. I think you will find some help here. A lot of the material I use in the book was taught to me by other more experienced teachers, or by students.

I have divided the book into Chapters dealing with Administration, Staff, the physical classroom and classroom control, and Students. Sometimes a topic will fit into a couple of these chapters and I have just placed it where I think it will suit most. I have included a run down on each year level you will come into contact with in the 'Students' section. I make some observations that can apply to that year level, but of course, you are always going to get individuals who just will not be categorised like that. However, it does make it easier to divide up the book. You might disagree with some of the things I say, or you might think some things need to be in a different chapter and that is fine.

I mostly teach English and Media Studies so I will be limiting any curriculum based observations to those two areas...As well as a bit of Humanities.

And I will probably digress at times. My students tell me I am prone to this. Just for information's sake I have also taught Business Management and Personal Skills.

I would like to take this opportunity to thank my wife and some other people who made my career in teaching possible. So, many thanks to ...

Kathy Higgins for supporting me as I studied and as I found my way in teaching.

Cynthia Grima who was my mentor and who taught me so much about teaching and who then continued to teach me as a friend.

Jenny Price who also gave me much useful advice about teaching from a completely different perspective from Cynthia.

Jo McInerny who showed me the importance of passion in teaching.

And of course all of the other teachers and students, support staff and others that I have crossed paths with over the years. Some of you will see yourselves in these pages, but its ok, I don't name names.

In The Classroom

You don't just teach.

It was only while making some preparatory notes for this book that I realised what a varied amount of information I am going to have to convey. In many jobs, it is simply a case of 'do this, then this, then this. Then go onto to the next one. Although of course that might have just been the jobs that I was involved with ages ago. Anyway, I kept making notes about things I thought I should discuss and each idea threw up a few other topics and I ended up with a list of things that I needed to address that were so disparate, it was hard to get my head around how to order them. And then I realised that this was a perfect way to describe the typical teaching day. I was then tempted to just write about each aspect of teaching as they appeared on my list of things to tackle, and it would look clever and cool and I wouldn't have to actually maintain some sense of order. If the reader couldn't follow the flow of things, that was their problem.

It then occurred to that making things difficult to understand in what is essentially a guide book about teaching probably was not the best way to go about it. So I have ordered things. They are not according to importance because honestly, one day good planning will be important and the next day, making sure you get a decent night's sleep will be top of the agenda. Actually, that could occur in one lesson rather than one day, so hopefully you will get my point. Welcome to teaching.

Accelerated Classes

Once upon a time, only a few schools in the state of Victoria, offered accelerated classes.

My school was one of the first public schools to offer this form of learning and it meant we were able to attract students from a very wide area. Prospective students sat an aptitude test and were then invited to enrol in our accelerated program depending on the results. They could have been proficient in English and offered a place on that basis. Or they may have been good at maths and that would see them enrolled. Often we got a dud student in the accelerated English and we just assumed they were fantastic at Maths because it sure wasn't their English skills that got them in.

Our Year 7 Accelerated class operated at Year 8 level and so on up until Year 11 where they joined the mainstream and coasted for a year until the rigours of Year 12 made them work to their potential.

Teaching the Accelerated class was a two edged sword (aren't all swords double edged?) On the one hand their behaviour was usually fantastic. They were bright, engaged students who were like sponges when it came to knowledge and wanted to know everything about everything. The downside was that they wrote a lot. If you asked for 1000 words you got 2000. They did every assignment, all the homework, and it all had to be marked. Generally it was mostly good quality as well. So, fun to teach, bad to assess.

The parents of accelerated students always turn up to parent Teacher nights and you really have to be on the ball when discussing their children and their educational progress. They are very, very interested in how their children are performing. If you have any bad behaviour these parents will nip it in the bud. You get the occasional parent who thinks their progeny can do no wrong, but generally they recognise that kids will be kids and they will support your decisions.

Very occasionally we have dropped a student from the accelerated program based upon their performance and progress, but mostly they see school all the way through.

The program also means we get parents enrolling their children into our mainstream program in the hope that some of the accelerated student's work ethic rubs off. It doesn't. These days most schools will offer an accelerated program and they are called all sorts of names but they are essentially the same.

<u>Awareness</u>

I thought I had better put this in now as it is really important and it starts with 'A'. Much of what I will discuss calls for you to be aware of what is going on in the classroom. Early in your career you need to develop classroom awareness.

You need to actually scan around the room looking to see what it going on. Not just when you are delivering instructions straight to the class, but ALL the time. It is easy to get caught up in a one to one session with a student who is struggling with a concept, but you need to always look up and look around. In the long term this actually helps with classroom management overall as students will come to realise that you have your finger on the pulse of the class. As you scan the room just make a couple of observations based on what you see.

"Marty I thought we had an agreement that you were going to stop chatting.'

Then back to helping the struggling student.

"Emma, I could have sworn I just a mobile phone, but that can't be right as you are not allowed to have them in class.'

Then back to the struggling student. Honestly, the students will recognise that you are on top of the game and they will know that it is unlikely that they will get away with much.

<u>Breaks from class</u>

You will have students leave for the class for a lot of reasons.

-Toilet breaks and drink breaks. (I often get students who ask if they can "go to the toilet and get a drink" and I always say 'No. That's unhygienic')

-Music lessons. Schools often provide individual music lessons

- To get a pen. I always have spare pens, and they should be bringing one as a matter of course anyway

- To get a book. I allow this once or twice and then apply the need to make up the time

- To get their laptop. As above

- To get a charger for their laptop. I always have a spare.

- Sometimes you will get students organising to meet other students during class in the toilets or somewhere else. They do this via their laptop or their phone. If you notice a student who always needs to go somewhere at the same time each lesson, they are probably meeting others.

- Headache, cut finger, sore arm etc. Send them to the sick room.

- Have to go to Welfare. This could be a real need, or it could be a way to go meet friends. I think it is best to err on the side of caution and let them go, but email the welfare staff and see if the need was real.

Never allow more than one student out of the room at a time. They will go off and have a great time annoying other classes probably. If you really have to let a couple of students out, make sure they are not friends with each other.

<u>Choosing your Battles</u>

You will not win every adversarial encounter with a student. I know we would like to think that as trained adults we WILL win every encounter, but it isn't so. Sometimes teenage angst wins over wisdom and experience. You need to recognise when it is going to be a good idea to just walk away from a confrontation, or avoid the confrontation. When you see 'Emma' with her phone out you can choose to gently admonish her as described elsewhere, or even just make a general observation about the schools rules on phone use without even mentioning anyone by name or you can be heavy handed...

"Emma. You have got your phone out. Hand it over this instant!"

"You can't take my phone. It is MY property.'

"It is a school rule Emma. You know that."

"It's a dumb rule. What if my Nan is sick and My Mum needs to contact me?"

"Your Mum can ring the office."

"Well you are not getting it. You can exit me if you want." And with that Emma sticks the phone in her pocket and glares at you, daring you to argue further.

By now of course the whole class is watching to see how this plays out. But you have already lost. You are not going to get the phone handed to you, so you seem weak in the eyes of the class. Also, you are going to need to get the duty teacher to take Emma to the office where a member of the leadership team will deal with the situation which again leaves you looking weak in the eyes of the class. Plus you now have a broken relationship with Emma.

Now I'm not saying always give in to students who are doing the wrong thing. But you need to pick and choose. By just pointing out to Emma that I know she has her phone out, I have let her and the class know that I am on the ball and keeping an eye on things. I have given her the opportunity to put the phone away without causing a huge argument that disrupts the entire class. I have got what I want.

Now I could also get her to stay behind and calmly point out that she knows it is against the school rules to have her phone in class, and she will probably agree and apologise. Then I might add that the next time I see it I will have to confiscate it. Emma will probably agree that this is fair and reasonable.

Then, when the next time occurs and frankly it probably will, Emma will smile ruefully and hand over the phone because she knows that the two of you have a tacit agreement about this problem. She will know you are being fair (let's face it you let her off the first time) and that this is a fair outcome.

Renowned Classroom Management guru Bill Rogers, uses the excellent example of encouraging a student to get to work and as you turn away, you hear the student swear.

You can turn around and let the whole thing develop into a slanging match, or you can pretend you didn't hear. Being a deaf old teacher has its plus points at times.

The end result is that you have got what you wanted in the classroom. It all adds to your reputation of being a good teacher.

<u>Classroom Management</u>

This is the big one. I bet a lot of people reading this have skipped straight to this section. That's ok. It is the topic that impacts all teachers. It can make or break careers. Hell it can make or break people!

What you are going to get out of this chapter is going to depend a lot on you, your school, your students and your school's culture. Some of the things I say are going to disappoint you and some will inspire you. They will disappoint you because I am not going to say, "Just do this and this and this, and you will have no classroom management issues." I'm sorry but it doesn't work that way. You may get inspired because I will tell you some things that you can do to improve your classroom management skills.

I have received an awful lot of advice over the years that has helped me in my classroom. The best piece of advice I got was 'Be yourself'. If you are not a natural disciplinarian, don't try to be. Kids see through that. If you are not a naturally laid back, easy going person who strangely seems to get their own way in the classroom, don't try to be. If you are not funny, don't try to be. These are of course, all personal traits. Is there something that you can control? Is there some aspect of classroom management that you can have influence on and use effectively? Yes there is. I suppose you want me to tell you what it is... ok. Content. Know your stuff. Be all over your subject. Know what you are meant to teach, how you are meant to teach it and make sure you can answer any question that the students are likely to throw at you. Again, students know if you are faking it. You will be surprised how much easier classroom management becomes when you know your subject. It is not the be all and end all, but it is important.

So, be yourself. But how do you know what style of teacher you are if you are just starting out? Well, by now you should know yourself. You should be aware of your strengths and weaknesses. Play to your strengths. I have taught English alongside teachers with radically different approaches to teaching. Some have been stern disciplinarians, and others have been jokey, easy going people. Some have been serious and studious, and others have appeared lackadaisical and seemingly uncaring. I've worked with introverts, extroverts, dreamers, sporty types. They have all been effective classroom managers. By the same token I have known stern disciplinarians who have been useless at classroom management. They have had kids hanging from rafters and bolting out of doors and being completely disrespectful. I have seen easy going, laid back teachers being totally ignored by students who are not engaged, not cooperative and not learning anything. So what is the difference? What is the key to managing a classroom full of teenagers who do not want to be there?

We will get to answer to that but first I want to discuss two aspects of this topic.

When I first got the job I have now, we had a student free day at the beginning of the school year. Two things happened that day that helped to shape my teaching career. The first was, before the day got under way the principal had a quick meeting with all of the first year teachers. There were four of us. He sat us down, looked at us and said "Every year, one teacher is the bunny. Make sure you are not the bunny this year". It scared the hell out of me. I didn't want to be the bunny. By the way, I took the 'bunny' to be a cricket metaphor. If you are someone's bunny, they control you. They have you beaten before you even begin.

So if you were the school bunny, you were going to have a hard time with the students. Anyway his warning worked as none of us that started that day became the bunny. I was too busy learning how to teach to notice who did become the bunny, but I am sure someone did. It was probably a second year teacher.

The second thing that happened that day was the school had organised the then guru of Classroom management to visit the school and talk to us. His name is Bill Rogers. I remember taking copious notes. I also remember actually using a lot of what he said in my first few classes. The man is a genius. I tried to look him up online and it seems his webpages are now defunct, so I'm not sure what is going on there. However, there are still many YouTube clips of Bill in action giving little lectures on how to deal with difficult students. I strongly recommend you look at them and also order some of his books.

Rapport

I think rapport is the most important element of classroom management and I know I am not alone in thinking this. If you have built a rapport with individual students and with the class as a whole, that means you have developed a shared understanding with them. They know what to expect from you, and you know what to expect from them. In building this rapport, you need honesty.

I mentioned honesty earlier when discussing how to develop or identify your own teaching style. If you are not a natural disciplinarian, don't try to be one. Over a relatively short time, you will develop a rapport with your classes and with individuals in those classes, some more quickly than others.

In order for the students to know what to expect from you, you need to tell them and show them. Similarly, in order for the students to understand what you expect from them, you need to tell them and show them.

Most teachers, when encountering a class for the first time will set out their own classroom expectations. It is a boring way to start the term, but necessary. Remember you no not need to labour the point. Write your expectations on the board, and briefly discuss them. You can even point out that your class expectations are pretty much the same as other teachers' expectations, but go through them anyway. Plus it is a good idea to throw in one or two rules that other teachers do not mention. For instance, most teachers would write the following list of expectations;

1.Respect others

2.Respect other people's property

3.No phones

4.No games on laptops unless directly given permission

5.Hands up if you have a question

6.Do not talk when the teacher is talking

7.Do not talk when others are talking to the class

8.Ask permission before leaving the class or leaving your desk

9.Be on time to class

10.Bring the correct material to class

These are pretty basic rules that most students would be familiar with and it is what just about every teacher has told them. There are other rules you can throw in later. If I were facing a new class and wanted to go through these rules I would say the following;

"Ok, new class, so we better go through the rules. You will have heard these a million times before so it won't take long.

1.Respect others. Especially me. I am very shy and quiet and I hurt easily.

2.Respect other people's property. Especially mine! Leave my stuff alone. I'm only a poor teacher.

3.No phones...That is a school rule so I don't need to discuss that.

4.No games on laptops. I have a real thing about this, so consider this your only warning. If I see you playing games when you shouldn't I will have to replace your laptop with a book.

5.You need to put your hands up if you have a question... That's an oldie you should all know.

6.Ok now like all teachers I like the sound of my own voice, so don't talk while I am talking

7.And it is just good manners not to talk while others are talking.

8.Ask permission before you leave. That's just good manners again.

9.Be on time. I will be on time. The only time I will be late is if I get caught up somehow but you will find me here waiting for you %99 of the time. (If it is a year 7 class I will emphasise the fact that they won't be in trouble if they are late because they got lost. At the start of the year always give the 7s a bit of leeway).

10.Bring the correct material to class. If you keep forgetting stuff, I will have to get you to make up the time at recess.

That only takes a few minutes. You can then add a couple of personal rules. I always state that no one is to throw anything in my classes. I add that anyone seen throwing something, or mimicking throwing something, gets to pick up five pieces of rubbish from the floor. Don't worry there will always be something to pick up from the floor, and in the unlikely event there isn't, they can straighten the chairs at the end of the lesson. I generally explain that I once had a child throw a pen across the room in one of my classes and it hit someone in the eye. That's my justification for the rule. I stick to it even with senior classes.

The trick with all of these rules is to enforce the rules rigorously from the start. No exceptions. You can point this out to them as well. So even if it is your favourite class, and they have worked really well, if someone throws something you can act all disappointed. 'Oh no! You worked so well and then you forgot about throwing things. Five bits of paper please." After a while the students take it in good humour. Oh and if they pick up one piece of paper and tear it into five pieces, you up the quota to ten pieces of paper.

As you discover new wrongs to right, you can just say, 'Oh I just remembered a rule I forgot to mention at the start of the term. No food in class! It is a school rule but I forgot to mention it so I guess I won't make you share it with everyone this time. But no more, ok?'

I think that, if the students feel the rule is fair, and that you stick to it as well, they will generally abide by the rule. The catch to all of this is that YOU need to follow the rules as well. So whatever you do, turn your phone to silent in class.

So, what can the students expect from you? I go through this as well. You have expectations that they have to meet, so it is only fair that they know what they can expect from you. I write the following on the board and discuss each point.

1. I will treat you with respect. If I have a problem with your work or your behaviour, I will talk to you about it. If it is still a problem, I will talk to your Year Level coordinator. If it is still a problem, then I will talk to your parents. (Again, this smacks of fairness. Kids have a strong sense of what is fair and what isn't)

2. I will supply work that you can complete and I will try to make it interesting, however, let's face facts. We will be looking at punctuation/ fractions/economics etc. so there's only so much control I have over how boring it is.

3. I will be on time, and prepared. I expect the same from you guys, so it's only fair I give the same promise

And those two little exercises will be over in a few minutes. They know what to do, and they know what you will do. But you must stick to it. Do not be late the next lesson! Make sure you are prepared for the lesson. And keep it up. The most crucial thing here is routine and predictability. If someone swears, pull them up on it. Tell them it is disrespectful and, as the student knows, that is not acceptable. If you are not happy with someone's behaviour, ask them to have a quiet chat about it, or ask them to stay back for just 30 seconds to discuss it. Again, discuss what they have done wrong and point out it is not what was expected. Don't make a big song and dance about it. Remember, at this stage you are building a rapport. The students need to see you are serious about what you expect and that they can expect repercussions if those expectations are not met. If you are unable to get a satisfactory response from a student, by all means talk to their coordinator as you promised you would. If the problem is still not resolved point out to the student that, as per your promise at the start of the year, you will need to talk to the student's parents, then do so. And keep trying until you get a response from the parent. This certainty is worth a lot when it comes to your credibility. If you follow through, always, you will get a reputation as being firm, but fair. Students do talk about teachers.

Marty – Bloody Higgins told me he was going to talk to my folks. D'you reckon he will?

Jake – Yeah he will. If he says he is going to he does. He's a bugga like that.

The benefits of following up was sheeted home to me one lunchtime.

Previously I had told a student (Lets stick with Marty) that I wanted to see him at lunchtime and when the bell for lunch rang, he raced out the door before I could stop him. I wandered around the school until I found him. I sat him outside the admin office for ten minutes while I got a cup of coffee. I then sat and pointed out that if he had stayed to see me at the start of lunch, I would have taken up one minute of his time. Instead, he had now wasted about 15 minutes of his lunch. He apologised.

Some months later I stopped a student from doing something and told him I was wanted to see him at lunchtime. This student got a bit smart and said he might turn up. Whereupon Marty pipes up from behind me and tells the student, 'You better show up. If you don't Mr. Higgins hunts you down at lunchtime and keeps you in for ages." The student showed up. My work had been previously done for me.

So be clear about what you expect. Be clear about what they can expect. Stick to your rules relentlessly.

Some teachers maintain that you should never smile before Easter. It's an old idea and I know some people feel if they come across as scary then the students will know that they mean business from the outset and that they will not play up too much. I have a fairly happy disposition in class and I couldn't keep up that sort of performance for that long. Plus I think the kids would see through it anyway. Plus it doesn't work. If you have not developed some sort of rapport with your classes by Easter, then both you and the students are in for a long year.

Ongoing classroom management

Ok, you have a good rapport with your kids. They work reasonably well. They behave themselves mostly. They can be a bit chatty, but not so that you find it annoying. How do you keep it going?

Every interaction you have with classes as a whole and with individual students is going to be informed, or influenced by your existing relationship with them.

With minor instances of disrespect, I always sit with the student and calmly ask if I ever talk to them in a disrespectful manner. They point out that I do not. They are forced to say that because I never, ever do.

This is a really powerful way of talking to a student and discovering what is causing a problem. If they are forced to acknowledge that you treat them with respect, they are forced to treat you in the same way. Remember, kids have a strong sense of fairness. If you have treated them disrespectfully, well, you have no credibility. This is why it is crucial you remain fair and respectful at all times.

By all means point out that 'Marty' is a painful little smartarse in the staffroom. I will say more on this later but always remember what is said in the staffroom, stays in the staffroom. Teachers need a place to vent. But always be in total control in the classroom. You are the adult remember?

Other forms of disruptive behaviour

Ongoing loud chat by a lot of students – I had a system where I would ask for quiet. If the noise levels rose again I would point out that we might need to have a discussion at recess. If the noise remained at that level or increased, I would move to the right of the whiteboard, and write 'recess – 3 minutes' in the top right hand corner of the board. If the noise levels went up again or continued, I would slowly and deliberately cross out the 3 and change it to 4. If you keep increasing the time in small increments, you will get sections of the class who will start to police the noise. I.e. "Be quiet! He is going to put it up again!'

and most will comply. If they are really quiet for a period of time, I will rub out the 4 and reduce the time to 3, then 2, etc, because frankly, I didn't want to stay in at recess either.

You will get one clever one who talks loudly just to annoy the rest of the class and to force them all to have to stay behind. In that case you simply point out that you have decided that it isn't fair to keep the whole class in because one or two are being noisy, and you will just keep those noisy ones back. Problem solved.

Fights in class

Again, the well run classroom will not have many fights, but they do break out from time to time. If it is verbal, separate the protagonists a long way from each other. If it is still a problem, get both outside for a chat. If it still escalates, exit them. If it turns physical, get between the parties involved and raise your voice. Get someone to get the duty teacher, and calmly try to get the warring parties to back off.

If you are small of stature and you are dealing with big, Year 10 boys, you can still impose yourself bearing in mind that they will be very hesitant to hurt a teacher, or you can place a chair between them as a way of separating them.

I should talk here about the use of your voice. Use a raised voice as little as possible. If you yell at the students a lot, you have nowhere left to go. You cannot yell louder for impact if you generally yell loudly at them anyway. I have yelled twice at a student in the last twenty years. And no, it wasn't the same student.

Once was just to shock a boy into stopping what he was doing. (He was about to hit another student for a second time) and the other time was to get a student's attention.

We were on a Year 10 Camp in the city of Melbourne. Ah, the Year 10 City Survival Camp. Great times. We would go to the museum, MCG, Science works, Movies etc and the kids loved it. It was a full on, four day camp. On this particular night we were walking toward the cinemas located in the Crown Casino district. We were walking because you get the kids to walk a lot on these camps so you can tire them out. This particular evening was cold and rainy. I was bringing up the rear. I noticed one girl was standing in the middle of City road with four lanes of manic drivers keen to get home just getting a green light and heading toward her. She was stopped there examining her shoe which had come off her foot and was broken. I screamed at her to move but she just stood there oblivious, until I forcibly grabbed her am and moved her quickly toward the pavement.

That reminds me I need to include something about touching students somewhere. Don't do it unless not to do so would cause more harm, like if she was about to be run over by a car.

Anyway, altercations will occur. They will probably be sparked by something said in the yard at recess, or in the previous class and you need to be aware of them brewing so you can nip them in the bud.

Swearing

There might be a bit of this. Usually it is real low level stuff and it is really just the student forgetting where they are for a moment. If it is ongoing and really full on you will need to have a chat with the student. (I am always having 'chats' with students. They hate it). Generally I point out that I do not swear, and that it is not allowed in the workplace. In fact it is not allowed in any workplace. I tell them I am offended by the swearing and it really isn't fair to swear like that when I find it offensive. As I have pointed out, kids 'get' fairness. This is one of those times where you set the standard early in the year by telling the class you do not allow swearing in your class and you then stick to that rule and apply some form of penalty, such as five minutes in class at lunchtime or whatever suits you. If you have a yard duty you can always have a plastic bag and pair of disposable gloves handy and invite the offender to pick up ten bits of rubbish with you while you are walking around. Honestly, you only need to do this once or twice to enforce the rule.

Insults

You will have insults directed at you. Do try to remember that it isn't really personal. It is a bit like those mafia 'hits' in the movies where it is just business, and not personal. I don't suppose that is much comfort to the person on the receiving end of the business however. But do remember that the insult isn't really meant to attack you personally. It is just the student doing what students sometimes do. They are rebelling. You will probably find they will have forgotten about it shortly afterwards, or they will seek you out and apologise, and nine times out of ten they will let you know that they were just having a bad day. So, don't stress too much about insults.

Actually an insult provided me with my best comeback. A student told me I was the worst teacher in the school. I told him that would be too much of a coincidence. I probably should not have said it, but the temptation was just too great.

Leaning back in the chair

This is just a personal dislike of mine. Some kids are chronic chair leaners, especially when they are at the back of the class, against a wall. It can wreck the chair, but they can also lean back too far and have the chair slide out from under them. This can really damage the chair...Oh and the student. They can get damaged as well. I just give a warning and if it persists, I have special 'how to sit in a chair' lessons at lunchtime.

One year I had one student who just could not help himself. He leant back in the chair just as soon as he sat in it and no amount of reminders would keep him seated properly. So one day I had him pick up his plastic chair, hold it over his head, and instructed him to run to the middle of the adjacent oval. When he got to the middle he was to spin around three times yelling "I must not lean back in my chair", as loudly as he could, and then he had to run back to the classroom still holding the chair over his head.

He did it, much to the amusement of the rest of the class, and other nearby classes. I don't recall if this had the desired effect, but I think it must have as I don't recall it being a problem with him after that.

Things that influence student behaviour

Wow, where do I start? Or stop? If your students are behaving weirdly or slightly out of character it could be due to one, or a combination of these elements:

The time of day – students are generally better behaved in the morning, and get a bit ratty later on in the day.

The day of the week

Monday – Students might be refreshed or they might be angry that they are back at school

Tuesday – Generally a good day

Wednesday – Students can be a bit off as it is only Wednesday

Thursday – Gee this is a long week

Friday – unsettled for obvious reasons.

The week of the term

Weeks one to four are like Mondays

Weeks five to eight are like Wednesdays

Weeks nine to end of term are like Fridays

The Season

Summer (start of Year). It is hot, but the kids are excited to be back

Autumn – (Term 2) Kids can be unsettled. It's getting cold and dark. Teachers can be unsettled

Winter – It is all a bit moody and cold

Spring – Yay. The end of the year is approaching. The kids start to seem optimistic and happy (conditions apply).

So you will hear teachers explain the poor behaviour of students on the fact that It's hot/cold/ the start of the week, the middle of the week, the end of the week, or it's early in the term, late in the term, cold, dark, or too light etc. etc. etc.

The classroom set up

This can have a dramatic effect on students. If you have a particularly raucous bunch you might try separating all of the desks so that you have a gap between every table. This breaks up friendship groups and makes conversations difficult to have. It also means that some students will simply talk louder to their friends.

Some students will just begin to rearrange the furniture in a room to suit themselves. You need to stop this very early. You are the only person who is allowed to move tables. If I have set up a room differently to control behaviour, I always promise that they can have the room back the way they like it if I am happy with how they work.

The same is true for seating arrangements. Some rowdy classes will need to have set seating arrangements where they are not sitting with friends. You tell them the arrangements will be random, but you carefully decide who will sit next to whom and where in the room they will sit. Kids hate this, but it can be a very effective way to impose control on a class. And again, you can promise to revert to the usual way of seating if you are happy with their behaviour.

Current affairs

Major news events can have an impact on students. I did my rounds just before 9/11 and I know that event had a profound impact on many students. Some of them did not worry about it in the slightest, but some kids, like some adults like to catastrophise how an event impacts them and that sort of event will set them off.

Deaths in school

Thankfully I have not had to work through many deaths in the school, but there have been a couple. I have had student suicides and accidental deaths to work through and it is always a dreadful time. The students tended to go very quiet and contemplative. Death by suicide in schools is taken very seriously because of the tendency for students to copycat the death. Sadly one death can lead to another in the same area.

The education department are very good at organising counselling for students and staff, and the welfare department in schools tends to step up even though it is obviously a very busy time for them.

Fortunately, I have not had to deal with the death of a close colleague in a school although I have had a couple of ex fellow teachers pass on. In a tight community these deaths do have a flow on effect and do obviously impact many people. Students are going to react differently to these events and of course, they are also going to experience death in their own families. Your welfare staff will be the best ones to approach for advice on how to support students going through these difficult times.

Immunization days

These only apply to junior classes, and they can be an ordeal (I mean for teachers. We already know it is an ordeal for the students). You will get kids freaking out over the thought of a needle and you will get other students needling those students (if you get what I mean) and making them even more agitated. Fortunately these days are usually organised so the needles are in the morning and the kids get over their worries pretty quickly. But remember, for some kids the fear of needles is extreme. Leave it to the nurses and welfare to sort out the real problems. But it can be a prick of a day. Sorry.

Photo Day

The day where everyone has fluffed themselves up to look their best. It can be a bit disruptive as classes are called out by year levels, cat herding ensues, and then everyone goes back to their room all settled and content to continue with their learning. Or not. Your school will have devised a way to keep all of this moving efficiently so as to cause the minimum disruption to classes. Or not.

Casual Clothes Day

This one seems to have an extraordinary impact on the students. Generally a causal clothes day will be called by the Student Representative Council and it will be used to raise funds for a cause or charity.

Students can come in casual clothes and they have to make a gold coin donation during form assembly.

Junior female students are advised that low cut tops coupled with a piece of cloth accurately named 'shorts' is not really what casual clothes are all about. This sort of get up is de rigour for junior girls even if the casual clothes day is being held in mid-winter. The boys tend to wear jeans and a top. Anyway, they all go a bit crazy because they are dressed differently. This is normal teen behaviour.

The wind

Some teachers swear that children are badly behaved on windy days. They are, but they are also badly behaved on still days and on slightly breezy days. So I guess technically they are right, but....I'm not sure on this one. Full moon yes. Absolutely... but wind?

More thoughts on Classroom management

You are probably going better than you think. I was told this early on when I was worrying about my future employment. We had a Principal who kept pretty much to himself mostly. I was chatting with another first year teacher and he asked me if the Principal ever spoke to me. I said no. He didn't even say 'Hi' when I passed him in the corridor. My first year friend had the same experience, so we both decided that neither of us would be there long. After a while we discovered that this was just the way the Principal was and that he thought we were both doing a really good job. I guess if we had been stuffing things up, THEN he would have talked to us.

If in doubt, talk to your mentor. If you do not have a mentor, get one. This should happen early. A good mentor is crucial to the success of a new teacher. Our mentor program slipped a little while ago, and people were just taking it upon themselves to mentor new teachers, or struggling teachers, out of the kindness of their hearts.

Most schools will assign someone to you. The key to being a good mentor is to make sure that your Mentee feels comfortable asking questions. You know what it is like when you start a new job. You just think everyone is going to get sick of you asking dumb, basic questions all the time. And they probably do get sick of it but ask them anyway.

One day you will be getting asked those questions. The key to being a good mentee is to ask lots of questions even if they are dumb questions.

Always remember that if you have an awful class, you will be worrying over it for ages. It will play on your mind for the rest of the day. You will wake up at 2 in the morning going over the class and pondering its implications. How bad are they going to be next time?

Is this the end of my teaching career? Will they tell their parents who will complain to the school that I didn't know how to control the class? The students on the other hand have probably forgotten about the class by the time they hit the last of the three steps on the way out.

Don't make assumptions about students. If someone tells you that 'student A' is a real nasty piece of work, try not to treat them like they are until they demonstrate their poor behaviour to you. Students do change and most kids at the start of the year will be trying to make a change for the better. You will witness some remarkable changes in personality during your career. This is a time of great change for these children and some of the changes will be... well great.

I once had a Year 9 female student who was hard work all year. I was dreading having her again in Year 10, but gave her the benefit of the doubt and I pointed out to all of the class that this was a good year to make a fresh start in their studies. My ex year 9 girl was fantastic. Hardworking, cooperative, responsible and polite. That was one parent meeting I was looking forward to when it came to Parent Teacher interviews, and the girl's parents were thrilled.

An added bonus for teachers is that, for some reason, colleagues and weirdly parents, credit you, the teacher, for this turn around. Make sure you give the credit to the student when this occurs.

By all means contact home when you need to do so. Try to sort out problems with the student first, and with their form teacher or coordinator if required, but then, if necessary talk to Mum and Dad or their guardian. Most times, but not all sadly, this will have a very powerful impact on a given student's behaviour. When it doesn't have any impact, well you need to feel sorry for the student because it may mean that they do not have parents who care about their education.

I rang home once to point out that a student had not completed his homework and was behind on his major assignment.

His mother said I should deal with it and not to bother her. Some parents just do not care. It happens.

On this same topic, if a student is constantly trouble, and they are willingly disruptive and just seem to be looking for trouble all of the time, their home life is probably really shitty. Just bear that in mind when you are dealing with them. Your attention might be all the attention they get.

Oh and don't forget to occasionally ring home to praise a students work. One of my happiest memories came from one of these calls. We had a troublesome student called, oh hell lets go with Marty again. Marty was in my Year 7 form group and I had him for English. He was low level annoying. He'd talk, annoy other students and generally be a dick. I had him again in Year 9 and his behaviour hadn't improved any. He was of course by now, a bit naughtier and a bit more brazen with it. He was always getting exited from other classes. He wasn't too bad for me. The fact that I had him in Year 7 meant I had been able to build a relationship with him.

Once, in year 7 he was exited and I was the duty teacher. He knew he had stuffed up, and he was remorseful. He didn't want to be put in a Year 12 class for the rest of the class and he started to cry. I felt sorry for him and sat him outside my staffroom with a book to read. He never forgot that and we had a fairly good working relationship. Well I worked, and Marty didn't do much of anything. He just hated schoolwork. But, one day I convinced him to do some work. I said if he completed the set work I would give him a green Compass entry, which basically meant his parents would be able to see that he had done well.

That worked for a while, but then he fell back into his old ways and didn't do much. Then, I told him if he completed an assignment, I would enter a positive comment on Compass. He asked me if I would also call home. Little did I know that Marty was in trouble at home for some misdemeanor, but I agreed. Marty did the work.

I called home and spoke to his dad. As soon as I identified myself and said I was ringing from the school, Marty's father's voice fell. I could hear him thinking, 'Oh God. He has stuffed up again. What is it this time?' I pointed out that I was ringing to tell him that Marty had worked well that day, and he had completed his assignment. You would have thought I was ringing to tell him he had won the lottery. He was almost in tears and told me I had made his day. I just said that we often rang for bad reasons and it was only fair that Marty got some deserved praise. So remember to ring home for good reasons as well.

If students are constantly late, keep them in after class. If you get your students in the habit of thinking class time is important, you will be able to reason with them that any time they miss through lateness, will need to made up during a lunchtime. Again, if you do this and stick to it to a few weeks early in the year, you will have solved this problem before it has become a problem.

<u>Content – What you teach</u>

I am going to have to make a few general remarks about this as clearly I am not in a position to talk with any authority about all the different study areas. I do not want to alienate teachers in other areas, by just going on about English and how that is taught, no matter how beneficial English teachers would see that as being.

You must have lesson plans. They must be detailed and ideally you will have developed a few of them with other members of your KLA (Key Learning Area) who are teaching the same year level as you. If your KLA does not have this level of collaboration you need to create it. Sit down with your mentor and develop lesson plans with them. Partner up with someone who is new like you and develop lessons plans with them, then show the plans to your KLA leader. Your school will have a lesson plan pro forma. Trust me they will. No one will know where it is, but it will be around somewhere.

Also, the department has study designs that detail what you should be teaching. You can go online, download these, and then, again collaborating with a friend, you can attempt to translate them into something that is understandable and useful. You think I'm joking? Go and read one. If it all makes perfect sense to you then you are in the wrong job. You should be an administrator, not a teacher.

There will be an organisation that supports your area of study. Some of these are better than others.

The two that I have had experience with are good examples of the extremes you can get in terms of quality. I mainly teach English and Media Studies. The organisation that supports teachers of Media studies is called, unsurprisingly, Australian Teachers of Media or ATOM. I have been to a few professional Development days run by ATOM and they were fantastic. Well run, well organised and useful.

I came away with tons of ideas for future classes and tons of resources that supported those future classes. They had knowledgeable speakers who had shared tried and tested classroom material, ideas and techniques. Plus, they had really good food.

The organisation that supports English teachers is the Victorian Association for the Teaching of English (VATE). See, they don't even have a catchy acronym! I went to a few days organised by VATE. The absolute worst was held at a high school about two hours' drive away. There were about twenty people in attendance including four from my school.

The guest speaker, an experienced Year 12 teacher, was there to talk about teaching year 12 English. Her opening remarks were "I want the content today to be driven by your needs, so please, let me know what you want to know.' Any experienced teacher will tell you that this is code for "I have not bothered to prepare anything for today. I am going to wing it and hope I can generate discussions from your suggestions.' It was a complete waste of time.

Some of the VATE days were ok, but they were mainly concerned with the study of a given text that we were looking at and, as such, were very specific in what was required of the presenter. I.e. Knowledge of the text. I sincerely hope VATE has got its act together. I honestly just gave up attending VATE professional development so they may have improved.

Online Content – Be very wary about developing lesson plans based on online material. Some of it is good, some of it is bloody awful and a lot of it is just ok. This is probably a reflection of the teaching skills of both the people who upload it and the people who download it. Much of it will be very generalised. A lot of it will be dated.

After a while you will get to know who in your KLA brings this sort of substandard material to the table when you are all contributing material for a shared year level class. The best material is developed by teachers who know their students, and if there is one of these in your KLA, make sure you befriend them. And if you use their material, credit them for creating it. Also, importantly, make sure you also contribute material that you have developed sometimes. Your fellow teachers will not be expecting you to create resources straight away. They will share their stuff with until you demonstrate that you are a taker and you are not contributing anything.

By all means use online content as a basis for the material you supply to a class, but try to avoid just downloading any old rubbish and hope it works. It probably won't.

New teachers (and some old teachers) are not confident about sharing the material they create for their class with other teachers. They are afraid that it is not of a high enough quality, or it isn't relevant or it just isn't relevant or it is really bad. And frankly, this is likely to be the case sometimes, especially early in your career, but share it anyway. Point out it is bloody awful. Say you are embarrassed to show it. People will make supportive noises and they will either suggest ways to improve it, or they will agree and say it is awful. If the former you will end up with improved material to use in class. If the latter you will learn how to create better resources and, if you are lucky, you will be given some decent resources to tide you over.

Most KLAs will have a central shared resource folder. My old English department used to have a huge four draw metal cabinet that was stuffed with worksheets, assignments, words searches etc. Then this got converted into digital places where people can add their own resources, or share resources they have found online. It is always a good idea for a group of subject teachers to appoint someone to keep the shared resource space tidy.

If you are a new teacher and you find that your colleagues are not sharing resources, pester them because they should. If you are an experienced teacher and you find that your colleagues are not sharing resources, then start sharing some yourself. Remember that what works for one class might not work for another and that any resource you use might need to be altered slightly to suit your students. And it might need to be further altered to suit the needs of individual students in your class.

While I am on this topic, you also need to remember that what you have used before successfully might not fly the next time around. This is true of assignments, worksheets, activities and texts. I once had two Year 9 classes of pretty much the same ability level in the same year. So on a Monday I might have had 9A in period 2 and 9C in period 3. Some activities worked for both, but not many. Sometimes I had to radically alter some assignments for one class. It was really weird. Usually having two classes the same like that is good as it does cut down the lesson preparation, but not always.

Also, sometimes you will spend a lot of time and effort in writing up a fantastic unit of work, or even just one lesson. You will enter the classroom enthused and confident that not only are the kids going to learn a lot, they are going to have fun doing it! Well, be prepared to change at a moment's notice. You will look around the room after you have explained the task, and you will be getting blank expressions, whinging and total disinterest. No matter how well you sell it, it is not going to work. Always be prepared to do something else. It is not a sign of failure that you need to change the lesson plan, it is a sign that you can recognise when an idea isn't going to work.

Some teachers will just plough on as they will not want to waste all that preparation. That doesn't make them bad teachers. We have all done it. I am just saying be prepared to change your mind.

Exits

I have not had to exit many kids during my career. I like to think that it is because I can talk kids around, but maybe it's because I haven't had many difficult kids? No, on reflection it is because I can talk kids around. I think the important thing to remember about exiting a student for poor behaviour is that it should not be viewed as a failure on the part of the teacher. Ok, sometimes I have seen or heard of teachers exiting kids for little reason, or as a pre-emptive strike based upon previous behaviours. Generally however, I think most teachers exit because it is the last resort.

Always start off with the lowest, most moderate response.

"Marty, you keep talking when I'm talking. Can you be quiet please?"

"Marty, I have asked you to be quiet. Would you like to move to this chair near me?"

"Marty I didn't move you there so you could have a long distance conversation with Kevin. Step outside where we can have a chat."

"Marty, I have tried everything to get you to settle and you leave me with no alternative than to exit you. If you do not settle, you will be exited.'

"Ok Can we have someone go and get the duty teacher please.'

Sometimes you do need to exit a student for everyone's sake including the student.

Your school will have a procedure in place for the exiting of students, so make sure you know what it is and follow it. Generally you will need to send a trusted student to go and get a duty teacher who will then come and collect the offending student and take him to a senior class, or to a designated supervised room.

Mostly I was able to get students to settle by having a chat with them outside of the classroom but this was only after I had built up some sort of relationship with the student. They knew I wouldn't exit them for no reason, and we could be honest enough with each other that the student would own their behaviour.

If you have a student who wants to be exited, you can try the following.

Institute a class rule early in the year that means any time missed from class because of exits needs to be made up at lunchtimes. I had one student who constantly wanted to be exited as it meant he didn't have to do any work. At the time, students were exited to a year 12 class and the year 12 teacher rarely had the time to strictly supervise some year 8 kid who had been deposited into their class.

One day I had to exit the student when there was still thirty minutes of the period left. I made sure that he made up that time in the next lunchtime. That worked for that student once I had kept him in at lunchtime two or three times and from then on the threat of being exited had a real consequence for him. It also had a flow on effect to other students, both in that particular class, and in my other classes. Word gets around. However, you have to follow up and actually go through with it, which means you miss a couple of lunchtimes as well.

But this is worth it if you have regained a useful persuasive technique in managing that one student. Well more than that one student actually because he will certainly tell his friends. Your reputation will then be enhanced as that teacher who always follows up.

The 'Look'

You will develop a 'look' that you will employ at times when you are deeply unhappy about something a student is doing. My wife says that I have deployed it against her once or twice and she did not like it at all. She said she has seen me use it with pesky sales people or anyone who is annoying me as well. I am usually aware when I use it, but sometimes I use it unknowingly.

It is a fantastic weapon and students will recognise it when you use it. It is best used with a quiet voice for maximum effect. As mentioned elsewhere, teachers who shout regularly at students leave themselves with nowhere to go. But a quiet voice can do wonders, and coupled with the 'look' it can be a game changer.

The look is part frown, part 'serious 'face and often delivered with a little side glance. It is hard to describe but your students will know it when they see it and you may not even have to utter a single word to get them to stop whatever they are doing. Perhaps practice developing your own look in the mirror? Actually it is probably better to let it develop naturally as your face will fall into that pattern better without you having to think about it.

I have often coupled The Look with a little side to side shake of the head to indicate that a student should not do what he is thinking of doing. This is incredibly effective as the student comes away thinking that you are a mind reader, when in reality, you just know how they operate.

Oral Presentations

Most students hate these. I can remember being at school and hating the idea of being asked to speak in front of the class too, so I can sympathise. However, they remain a part of the curriculum and I think they are a worthwhile skill to have under your belt. Some students will outright refuse to talk in front of the class which is bloody odd given these particular students often have no trouble talking all the rest of time. In fact is really difficult to get them NOT to talk sometimes.

There are some good ways to get them through this reluctance to speak in public. These can range from simply getting nervy students to come and chat with you while everyone is busy. While they are there with you just get them to look around at the class as they are engaged on something else. This is an unusual view for most students. When they are talking with you at your position in front of the class, they are focused on you. Once you focus them on the class, they can start to get a feel for how it looks.

While I'm at it, it is also a really good idea to sit yourself among the students every so often as well. You get a good feel for classroom dynamics when you are in amongst it.

Tell the students to carefully listen and look at what their other teachers are saying and doing in the classroom. This will be a new experience for some. Remind them that teachers are delivering oral presentations every lesson, every day. Some are better at it than others, but tell the student to observe their teachers carefully. Look for hand gestures; body language, use of props etc. listen for pauses, and changes in volume to add emphasis.

Remind the students that the best way to master Oral presentations is to know the topic and to know it well enough to be able to talk about it without the need for copious notes.

But do remember, some people have a real fear of speaking in public. Do not just dismiss this fear out of hand. Try to make things as easy as possible for the student to succeed.

You will get students who will say they will do the presentation but just for you. I generally compromise and get them to do it for me, and the other three of four students who do not want to give it in class time. It costs you a lunchtime but it does add to your relationship with the student. And if they are misbehaving at any stage, you can always tell them you are reconsidering your agreement to let them present at lunchtime. As they say, blackmail is a dirty word, but it is accurate.

The Performance aspect of teaching

Any teacher will tell you that the performance part of the job is both very important, and often neglected when people describe the role of teachers. Every day you will be putting on a series of performances to a critical audience. Imagine stage actors being asked to perform five or six times a day, in front of a crowd who doesn't want to be there, for not a lot of money, five days a week. Plus you have to write your own script for part of each performance and improvise for the other part. You need to be able to perform in that manner five days a week, and for forty weeks of each year. This performance aspect of the job comes as a surprise to many people and it is better to be aware of it than not. It can be tiring.

During these performances you will find yourself repeating some of your best lines every so often, however, if you have worked out a 'script' that works for that generic 'difficult Year 9 class' be prepared to change it as it might not work with another Year 9 class. I think it is probably the same with actors. Sometimes the material just does not go down as well as you thought it would.

So if you are going to be performing, let's have a physical appraisal of the place you are going to be spending a lot of time in for the next few years.

<u>Routine</u>

Managing a class is easier when you have bedded in a set routine for your class. Most students expect a routine and most thrive with a routine. Remember that sometimes, school life is the only part of some students' world that is ordered and predictable.

You could do something like this. At the time we had three 75 minute periods for English per week.

Monday – Silent reading for ten minutes (This was a part of our English KLA policy)
-Copy down this week's spelling words
-Begin work on whatever text or skill we are looking at
-Homework handouts

Wednesday – Silent reading

-Work on text or topic that is being studied

-Reminder about homework and spelling words

-Journal writing

Friday – Silent reading

-Spelling test

-Work on text or topic being studied

-Collect homework discuss the spelling test words and go through the results.

And despite the fact that I said students enjoy routine, you can and should change aspects of this occasionally. Life isn't all routine and sometimes it is good to get kids out of their comfort zone. However, I would certainly start with a simple set of tasks for all of the first term. Then after a couple of weeks reasserting the routine in Term 2, you can throw in a change.

Of course change will probably be thrust upon you when your school schedules sports days and photo days etc.

The School

If you are new to teaching, your only real point of reference is your own experience of school. Most schools are similar, but there are differences that might determine whether it is a 'calm' school or if it has some problems.

Obviously Private schools are going to be quite different to public schools, and I will be confirming my comments to the schools I have had experience in, which were public.

It you are about to start work in a new school, or have secured an interview at a school, have a walk around the school when there is no one there. Is it clean and tidy? Do the rooms look good? Are there dark and dingy areas? Obviously you can tell more about a school when there are kids actually in it, but it doesn't hurt to get a feel for the place. It sounds good in an interview if you can say you have had a wander around the place beforehand.

Do you remember how I said I can get distracted and go off on tangents? I want to talk a bit about job interviews. Let's just assume you have written a great application letter and included a wonderful CV, and you have been invited for a job interview. You will be nervous. It can be a daunting activity.

My first application was for a one year contracted position at the school where I had completed one of my placements, so I was a known quantity. I completely stuffed up the interview because I did not sell myself. Let's face it; the whole thing about a job interview is for you to convince the prospective employer that you are the right person for the job. For some reason I went with the honest answer approach. When asked what I knew about lesson preparation I just said, 'Not a lot, as we didn't really cover that much in my course.' I then pointed out that I would seek help from more experienced teachers.

That was pretty much my stock answer to all of the questions. I thought the interview panel would be impressed with my honesty. They were not. I didn't get the job. So, my advice is to find out as much as you can about teaching and THEN sell yourself. Really lay it on thick. If they catch you out with a tricky question, then you can go to the 'I'll ask experience teachers' option. Mind you, these days schools give job applicants a copy of the questions that they will be asked, so that makes it easier. But they can always throw in a tricky one.

Let's assume you have passed the interview and you have been offered a job. If you get the chance, visit the school when it is up and running. You will want to get signed into the system and borrow books from the library so there will be plenty of opportunities. As you walk around the school be aware of how it feels. Is it a calm school? Are there lots of kids roaming around unsupervised? Are any students freaking out for whatever reason? Are any staff freaking out for that matter. Where are the staff toilets? Is the school tidy? Where is the canteen? Does the food look good? Actually, the canteen and the standard of the food should have a whole category to itself. But that might just be me.

Although, food is incredibly prominent in the life of a teacher. Well, English teachers anyway.

What are the classrooms like? Is it an old school? Are there new buildings? Classrooms can be really important. My school had a whole new building added. 8 classrooms, all with huge folding doors as walls, so they could be opened to make bigger spaces (this rarely happened) and a new, 'you beaut' design that meant you didn't need to have air-conditioning or heating. The new system would ensure a constant comfortable temperature. After the school added air conditioners and heaters, the folding doors were sealed up the place became useable. Anyway, you will learn which classrooms work for you as you go, but remember, more space gives you more places to move students.

While we are on the classroom, make sure you know how to use the TV that will be in the room. You will use it a lot and there is nothing worse than having a well-planned lesson go badly because you couldn't show the YouTube clip you wanted to show.

Technology

I can't see this having much of an impact in teaching... Nah just kidding. I think in terms of changes in education, this is the biggie. This is where I get to demonstrate just how much has changed in the last twenty years.

I started teaching full time in 2003. We had rid the school of blackboards (apart from one room which still has a blackboard today) and we used flashy new whiteboards and whiteboard markers. (We knew the chalk wasn't going to be a goer with the whiteboards.) If we wanted our class to watch a film, we had to book the TV room at the back of the library and we had to all squeeze into a tiny space. I can remember showing 'Breaker Morant' to my Year 12 English class. Teachers did not have laptops, unless they had their own one, but we were soon to get them supplied by the department. A few people had mobile phones, but not students. And no, I do not mean to imply that students are not people.

The changes in the use and abuse of technology have been amazing. The fact that the internet is an incredible source of information and that makes it a natural part of the learning environment. (Look at me sounding all educational there). Unfortunately the fact that the internet is an incredible source of distraction makes it the natural enemy of the educational process. It is a puzzle that very few researchers have been able to solve.

It is no good telling teachers that technology should not be feared and that it can be made to be a useful tool for educators. We know that. Some researchers take the most blatantly obvious observation, research it and then state the bleeding obvious about the observation. 'Hey you guys have all these teenagers in one room at the one time, you should teach them stuff!'

So how do we use technology effectively? Well you cannot do it 100% of the time with 100% of the students. When we set a 2000 word essay, we do not expect all of the students to write 2000 words. Some will write 500 and some will write 2500 words.

If I tell a class to use their laptop to research the Egyptian gods, I expect some of them to do this, and this only. I expect some to stuff around for about ten minutes until I catch up to them and get them to close the game they are playing. I expect some students to ask me if they can go and get their laptop, and I expect others to waste ten minutes of time asking people if they can borrow a charger cable before getting one from me. I expect one or two to not get anything done because they don't have a laptop at school, and when I give them a textbook, they leave it until there is five minutes left of class time to tell me they don't have a pen. Or paper.

I think the trick is to set your rules around laptop use and stick with them. Make sure you enforce them early.

"If I see a game on anyone's laptop, it gets taken away and you work from a textbook. No warnings. This IS your warning. When you have finished the work, I MIGHT allow some free time for games at the end of the lesson."

Make sure you actually shut down a laptop. Point out that they can use it again if they get some work done, but make them earn it back. The promise of free time if everyone gets their work done is a great motivator. They will appreciate it even more if they have earned the free time rather than just taking it.

You have to remember that some of these students are actually addicted to their laptop or phone. And that is not hyperbole.

I had a VCE media class and we looked at the issue of addiction to technology. The students kept an honest log of their usage and they were stunned by the results. One girl readily admitted she had an addiction to her phone. She kept it turned on at all times and had it under her pillow at night so she would be awakened by any notifications that came through.

I think most people will admit that they have some sort of need to use their phones and tablets. One only has to look around a public space to see how many people are looking at their screens to know there is an issue. I mean, I'm looking at a screen as I write this!

It seems to me that the control over the use of laptops in the classroom is the more urgent problem. It is not the laptops per se, but rather how they are used. Students have to learn to use them wisely. They have to learn how to research well and how to be discriminating in the material they take from the internet. They also have to know how to write well and how to integrate quotes and researched information. Of course they also need to learn how to minimise their game early so that they do not get caught.

The introduction and use of artificial intelligence (AI) is only going to muddy the waters more as there is no known outcome predicted on how it is going to impact education. Society as a whole is very reactive when it comes to the impacts of technology. People knew that the digital revolution was going to change the way we operate in many areas of society, but no one really knew HOW it was going to affect us. We were told that technology was going to revolutionise schools, but no one knew how that would happen and we had to make up responses as we went. We still don't know how technology is impacting students if truth be told. The same will be true of AI.

AI is already impacting how students write essays. I had a really early example of this when I had a student hand in a typed essay that was clearly not written by him. I checked the internet for similar phrases which is the go to first step. Many years ago whilst marking 'Macbeth' essays I came across an essay that seemed really familiar. I flicked back through the essays and found the one I wanted.

There were whole chunks of the essays that were identical. Not all of each essay was identical, but certainly there were significant parts that were. I typed a few sentences into Google and there was the essay in full.

Now these two students had at least tried to disguise their plagiarism, its just that they were unlucky enough to have independently used identical pieces of the source essay. I simply put both on a table in front of the two students and said nothing. I just looked at them. They both admitted to cheating.

Anyway, I digress again. I told the student who had handed in the essay that was clearly not written by him, and he said he just ran it through a grammar checker but that otherwise the work was his. This would be like me claiming that I did in fact just swim a world record and Olympic record time despite the fact that I have only really mastered the doggy paddle. I was unable to find the essay he submitted anywhere on the Net and I got him to rewrite the essay. By hand. In class. It was only much later when I started to hear about AI generated essays that I realised what that student had done. I mean, full marks for trailblazing AI essays, but no marks for not at least putting in some typos to make it more like his own work.

I suppose the upshot is that all essays will need to be completed by hand in class. It is the only way that one can be sure that the essay is not written by AI.

The flow on effect of this is that teachers are going to have to make students write more by hand so that they are physically capable of writing more by hand, if that makes sense. You can tell them that this is an unexpected result of the use of new technology.

Every few days I hear of new uses for AI. Just today I heard that we would soon be able to have real time translations of media in other languages. This would then spread to real time translations of conversations. And these translations would be in an AI generated approximation of the original speakers' voice. This clearly has implication in the worlds of diplomacy, entertainment, politics, and many other areas of cultural life. Some people have posited that we will have teaching conducted by one teacher being streamed to multiple classrooms across schools and even across countries. You would have a supervising adult in the room maybe, but who knows? The interviews in the final chapter of this book provide some teacher views on this topic.

The study on the impact of technology is being outstripped by the growth and development of the technology. It is just too difficult to predict how any given technological advance is going to impact any given area of life. I am aware that even including this small amount of information about AI is going to really date this book very quickly. If you are reading this and AI has been successfully integrated into the education system, just forget everything I just said.

Mobile phones

There are two schools of thought regarding the use of mobile phones in schools. Some people are totally against them and want to ban them not just from classrooms, but they want to stop their use during lunchtimes and other breaks. The other camp recognises that phones are here to stay and they want to explore ways in which students can be taught to use their phones in a responsible manner.

I once wrote an article for the Age newspaper which basically advocated the banning of phones in class. However, I have also encouraged the use of mobile phones. See how you need to be a flexible thinker in teaching? I taught VCE Media Studies at a time when my school had banned the use of mobile phones in class.

A major part of the course called for the creation of a media product such as a podcast, a photographic folio or a short film. Many students opted to make short films and the cameras in the mobile phones were considerably better than the cameras they could borrow from the school. I got permission from the principal to allow the use of mobile phones in that class.

The use of phones is easy for schools to control. The hard part is deciding whether you want to ban them or allow their restricted use. Both New South Wales and Victoria have introduced state wide bans on the use of mobile phones in schools, and you only have to visit any school in either of those two states to see how well that ban is going. Yes some schools are adhering to the letter of the law, but most are not. It has to be admitted that at present, mobile phones are not essential for classroom use. If you want to control their use totally there is only one way to do it. You have to ban the phones from class. And the only way to do this successfully is for it to be a whole school policy with buy in from every teacher and as many parents as possible. It also helps when the students are on board with it as well.

As mentioned elsewhere, I was once a part of a committee that developed a phone use policy for my school. We developed it, discussed it with staff (this is when meetings are useful) and implemented it throughout the school. It worked brilliantly until some teachers began to make exceptions, or to ignore phone use because that was the easy option. You just cannot do this.

A whole school ban on classroom phone use must be assiduously pursued.

The school leadership need to continuously apply pressure on all staff and students to adhere to the policy. Not just at the start of each term, but all term, every term. So many policies get introduced in schools that flourish for a term or maybe even two terms, before they just fade away.

Some argue that the policy has become 'embedded' in the school but it hasn't. It has become ignored and forgotten about. This is the fate of most of the 'annual' programs that the Department of Education forces schools to introduce each year.

Some schools use a pouch system where the phones are placed in a pouch and are accessed again at the end of the day. Some just have a blanket ban and the students need to keep their phone in their locker all day. That was the approach at my school. However, students just put the phone in their pocket and came to class with it. Often they would have music playing with the ear buds hidden under their hair. Some bright Year 9 kids realised that their lockers were within Bluetooth range of their ear buds and set up their music before class, and did the right thing and left their phone in their locker. Clever.

Whatever system your school chooses, they have to work at it to make it stick. Sadly many schools let the policy slide. The State government decreed that phones should be left in lockers and that worked for a little while state-wide, until, once again, schools just let it slide.

You need ALL of the teaching staff onside. They have to police it. Personally I don't mind if the students have their phones at recess and lunch. They can do what they like as long as they aren't filming anyone or bullying on social media. But keep them out of the classroom.

I know some students will moan about having to have their phone in case their parents ring and of course the rebuttal is that parents can contact the school office anytime. Some parents will complain as well.

You just have to make it a part of school policy. If parents or students do not agree with the school policy they are free to complain, or go to another school. But it must remain school policy.

I really do think the use of phones has contributed to the deterioration of some student's behaviour and it is an area that is reasonably easy to control.

Now, I tend to think that we are going to have to accommodate the use of mobile phones in class. I think that the long term banning of mobile phones in schools is not sustainable. It only takes one teacher to decide that students may as well have their phones with them to create a chink in the system. Teenagers are very good at finding and exploiting chinks in the system.

I have come around to the view that students need to be educated on the responsible use of their phones. This is going to be difficult. I am unaware of any research being conducted on this issue but I assume there must be something happening, I hope it is anyway. Students will quickly learn when and how they can use their phones in the workplace, so we might as well get them ready for that now. It is a part of the school's job to ready them for the outside world after all.

Cast your minds back. You are in school. All you have in front of you is a pen and paper. You are meant to be writing an essay, but it isn't due for submission for ages so you plenty of time to waste. So you draw patterns, and doodle. Some of your doodles will be quite creative. You are not meant to be using your pen and paper for this purpose, and you won't do it all of the time, but still, it is a misuse of your time and resources. I know mobile phones are a few degrees more insidious than the ability to doodle with a pen, but the comparison stands. If students are taught to use their phones for good, rather than evil, everyone will be happier. You will always get a small percentage who do the wrong thing, but let's face it, that is always the case.

One last thing... What happened to the idea that the teacher would be able to see what was on the screen of every laptop in the class? That was how laptop use was sold to us at our school. 'Oh there will be no worries about students being on inappropriate sites in class as you will be able to see every screen and you will be able to shut down any laptops that are being used for games or whatever.

That never really happened. I guess we just have to keep wandering around the room watching students minimise their screens as quickly as they can.

Textbooks

You will be pleased when your KLA leader announces that the school is going to put a new English, or Maths or Humanities' textbook on the school booklist. Our English department has not really used textbooks much. The English textbooks I have used have been useful for dipping into and creating worksheets but you would not want to stick to the use of a textbook for your entire course outline. The trap with textbooks is that you think you can get away with just saying 'read page 42 and answer questions 1,3 and 4 in your workbooks'. I mean, you can do that sometimes, for a part of the lesson but do not do it all the time.

When I have been teaching Media, the textbooks available have been fantastic. Very useful, interesting and well worth the outlay for the students (or their parents anyway). I obviously cannot comment on the usefulness of Maths and science textbooks. I do have a friend who has written Maths textbooks and I am sure that they are fantastic, but I haven't used them.

My main problem has been with Humanities textbooks. I have taught Humanities a few times over the years and the textbooks have been uniformly bad. They are often pitched at a much higher level of ability than our students, and I would say our students are average ability wise. They are huge books, and some small students really do struggle with just the sheer weight of the things. And, they are as dull as dishwater. I mean, these kids are studying Ancient Egypt and the books make it boring! Come on! Mummies, pharaohs, pyramids and tombs and they make it boring? I would not have thought it possible but some textbooks can make any topic boring.

My point is use textbooks wisely. Do not rely on them for all of your content. They are a good start, but students soon tire of teachers who just read from the textbook without any supporting activities or ideas. Mix it up a bit. By all means read sections from the book, and maybe even complete a few of the questions, but include some physical activity. You are studying geography? Measure and map the school! Archaeology? Conduct a 'dig' somewhere on the school grounds. Economics? Have the students create a business from the ground up. And actually let them run the business. We always have kids running car cleaning businesses that always do well.

And in case you have nothing, and you cannot think of a single thing to do with the upcoming lesson, you can always rely on the Three Step Plan. This is the lesson plan you think of when you are three steps away from the classroom door. I know you doubt it but one day you will be able to come up with ideas on the run. It just takes experience and that will come with time.

<u>Work Ethic</u>

If a student just will not work, give them alternate tasks. You will need to talk to them first though. Remember that the reason they are not working might be that they simply have no idea what they are meant to do. So make sure they understand the task. Then keep returning to them to make sure that they can actually complete the task. If it is a still a problem, choose some of the easiest parts of the task for them to complete.

Try to familiarise yourself with the abilities of individual students as early as possible. This is one way of circumventing the previous point. In my English classes, and in others classes in my school, we have students complete short writing tasks early in the year. We do not do these to fill in time or to ease ourselves into the teaching year. We do it so we can assess what levels the students are at, and in what areas they may need assistance. A short writing exercise lets you know what their written communication skills are like. It gives you information about their comprehension skills, spelling skills, handwriting, and their ability to order their thoughts. If you make them write a brief biographical piece, you also get to know some details about their life, like hobbies and interests. This again will be useful in making a connection with the students.

Administration

If you cannot do, teach. If you cannot do or teach, administrate.

I have worked in many fields, in many roles and have been employed by both the federal and state governments and within the private sector. I have never seen a job that more over-administered than teaching. It has got to the point where the administration of teachers actually hinders the teaching process. All of those programs, courses, ideas and seminars that are designed to improve teaching have the opposite effect. They hamstring teachers and lead to dull, uninspiring, generic, formulaic and ineffective teaching. Every worthwhile idea is pumped up so an entire day of Professional Development can be built around it. This means padding the original idea until it no longer resembles the zippy little applicable idea it once was, and it is now a dull, boring set of research results made into a professional looking PowerPoint with flashy animated transitions.

Many years ago I worked for the Department of Agriculture. It was a great job. We could have done with a bit more funding for various programs we wanted to get up and running, but by and large it was a great job.

Because we were based in a fairly remote location, some four hours from Melbourne, we were not really affected by bureaucratic nonsense. Until the department decided to change their name. Suddenly all of our spare funding went toward the huge cost of rebranding the department. I think we became the Department of Primary Industry. It meant certain projects had to be delayed or dropped, but we had shiny new letterheads to tell stakeholders that the project that might solve an issue for them had been dropped. The name changed again a few years later.

I have worked in the public service long enough to know that it can be a fantastic place to be. But I have also seen the incredible growth in the public service. The whole structure of the public service encourages growth. The bigger a department is, the more funding allocated to them. The higher up the food chain they go. Ministers are encouraged to force the growth of their own department. You end up with thousands of people having to justify their job. And many of those people are conscientious and hardworking. And many others are not. I once worked with a guy who operated an import/export business from his department desk. Now some people might argue that his little hobby job was just a sideline, but I'm afraid it was his departmental job that was the little sideline. His 'hobby' was his main source of income.

It has been said that the best way to improve the effectiveness of a publicly funded organisation is to halve its workforce. There is a lot of dead wood in most government departments. For many years you literally could not get sacked unless you committed some heinous crime, and even then, well who knows?

As you can probably tell I am a little bitter about the whole bureaucracy surrounding teaching. Anyway, here are some pointers.

Acronyms
There are lot of these.

KLA – Key Learning Area. This will be your main area of Teaching. English, Maths, Science etc

AP - Assistant Principal. Often someone who has come up through the ranks at a school. Usually have their sights on the main job of Principal

PD – Professional Development. You have to do a set amount of PD each year. Fortunately just chatting to your colleagues over a coffee can count as informal PD. Your school will also organise a day long PD where you can be bored out of your brain being enlightened about all sorts of wonderful learning strategies

LAC – Learning Action committee? Learning Action Cell? Leading administration committee?

YLC – Year Level Coordinator. A good one is your friend and enforcer. A bad one makes your job hard.

ECA – I'm not sure what this one is or was. We had a big enclosed sports area/hall that was called the ECA. Education and Community Area?

VCAA – Victorian Curriculum Assessment Authority

VCE – Victorian Certificate of Education

VCAL – Victorian Certificate of Applied Learning

SAT - School Assessed Task or SAC (School Assessed Content)

VIT – Victorian Institute of Teaching

Ah the good old VIT. This august body costs a mint to run, and is basically in charge of keeping a list of registered teachers. All teachers will have horrific tales of dealing with this mob. My own tale began when the VIT was but a few years old.

I had submitted all of my paperwork and my registration fee to the VIT. I had submitted it well before the due date and it was all correct. Weeks passed. I got called into the Principal's office where I was told my registration was about to lapse as I had not submitted the paperwork required. I did not have much time to comply (again) so I decided the best thing would be to hand deliver the documents myself.

I went to Melbourne. I should point out I live in rural Victoria so this constituted a day trip for me. When I found the address that was stated on all of the VIT material and website I discovered they had moved.

To the other end to the city. I caught a tram and made it to the very salubrious end of town and I have to say when I made it to the floor where the VIT was located I was very impressed. Well, not impressed so much as pissed off. They have the most magnificent offices you can imagine, with a view that is quite stunning. And my school still had rooms that needed heaters and air conditioners. I waited. There didn't seem to be anyone about. Finally someone turned up. I told them what I needed to do, and, after I waited a bit more, they got someone who handled that sort of thing. We got to the last document and the VIT staffer realised that I needed to have something witnessed before they could accept the paperwork. She decided to get someone who could do that. I waited. She came back with some guy who apparently could do what was needed however, and I pause here for dramatic effect, he had left his special stamp back in his office, and could I submit the papers again some other time?

I said I would prefer to get this sorted today.

He said his office was a long way away.

I said my home was considerably further and suggested we go to his office rather than to my home, so that I could return another day.

He did that Year 9 thing of sighing and rolling his eyes as he walked off to get his special stamp.

Anyway, two years later the same thing happened again. Only this time the Principal knew someone who worked in the department. This person took my details, and ten minutes later I got an email from the VIT saying everything was sorted. It's who you know.

I have heard horror stories from new teachers about the hoops that they are made to jump through in order to get registered with the VIT. I mean, you have just passed a university course that says you are now a qualified teacher, and you then have to convince some public servants to put your name on a list.

During the latest teacher shortage, I did hear tales of retiring teachers being told they would not have to jump through these hoops if the reconsidered and stayed in teaching. Those tales may be apocryphal, but they may not be as well.

I hate the VIT. And you will too.

AIP – Annual Implementation Plan

Every school has an Annual Implementation Plan and when you have been to a couple of meetings dealing with the Annual Implementation Plan you will begin to realise that surely every schools' Annual Implantation Plan is going to be pretty much the same. All schools want to improve their Educational Outcomes ™ and will want better VCE results. And they will all state this in their Annual

Implementation Plan. You will notice that I keep referring to the Annual Implementation Plan by its full name rather than by just its initials. I do this because you need to get used to hearing about the Annual Implementation Plan and you should begin coming up with strategies to cope with these meetings about the Annual Implementation plan. Just rolling your eyes and contemplating fates worth than death just will not cut it I'm afraid. Of course if you like data and charts you will love these meetings. I was always amused by people pointing out where the boxes and whiskers were in a chart and how important these things were to the success of our school program and I knew, with absolute certainty, that half the staff didn't have the faintest idea what was going on, and they were wondering what the hell whiskers had to do with anything. Something to do with CATS maybe?

The Annual Implementation Plan itself is one of the most useless documents used at the school. Actually I shouldn't say it was 'used' as it wasn't. We looked at aspects of it every so often in a meeting and then promptly forgot about it until we had another meeting about it.

Sometimes we had one of those day long Professional Practice Days based on the Annual Implementation Plan, and as soon as the presenter asked if that information was now clear in everyone's minds, we all adopted a serious look and nodded wisely. Until that guy from the Arts KLA asked a question and someone from the Maths department wanted to clarify a point.

TAMABICBBLT - There Are More Acronyms But I Can't Be Bothered Listing Them. There are literally dozens more acronyms for you to look at and learn. Collect the whole set! You can find a list online and your school will have even more!

<u>Community</u>

You are a part of the school community. It is nice to belong. The school is of course a part of the broader community and hopefully there will be interaction between the school and the local community.

My school prides itself on its community ties but I really do think schools could do more within the community.

For a couple of years our VCAL program worked on building pathways, steps and bridges in a local nature reserve. It was fantastic to be a part of and it gave the students actual work experience. The work they completed still stands today, which in the case of one major footbridge, is a handy thing.

We also had a program where students would visit the local retirement village and nursing home. This was very popular with both the students and the retirees. They would chat and the females would do the nails of the older ladies, and the boys would talk war with the older men.

We would get the occasional local speaker up, but that was about it. I'd like to see a lot more contact with local groups and services. Many individuals steer well clear of the local school. I mean it is full of scary teenagers! Who can blame them? I just think local people would get a better idea of what goes on in a school, if there were more contact between the two.

The Law

There are two ways in which the law is going to be a part of your life as a teacher:

1. You are bound by the law to behave in certain ways. You need to have the welfare and education of the students as a priority at all times. This includes out of school hours. If you see a child doing something dangerous out of school, you are expected to do something to prevent harm to the child. During school you are considered to be 'in loco parentis' which doesn't have anything to do with kids driving parents crazy. It means you take on the responsibilities of a parent when in charge of the students. If you fail in this duty of care you can be charged.

2. You might have the Police come to your school. This might be to deliver a talk on driving or drugs or problems. It might be that

they are investigating some incident. If they are there investigating any vandalism or issues involving the school, you would hope that the students get the message and don't participate in any of that behaviour in future.

The students will get very interested if a police car arrives at the school and they will be abuzz with ideas about what it could mean. The ideas will invariably be wrong.

Email

What, I hear you ask, about emails? Is education now enhanced by the wonderful ease of communicating ideas instantly and efficiently? Surely in this digital age just about everything can be done online and electronically. Well, yes it can, and it does. Everything does get done electronically as well as either in person or on paper. You will get millions of emails. And you will get tons of group emails and they will get duplicated when someone replies to a group email with just 'Thanks' in the body of the email, but you will get all of the original email that they just quoted. Then someone will reply to everyone on the email list, including the original body of the email, and quoting the person who said 'Thanks' simply to say that you shouldn't include everyone in the reply to email when all you are saying is 'Thanks'. Etc.

Plus, your school will use a program like Compass that manages reports, and timetables and allows for contact home. It's a really good program. But, when someone makes a post on it, you will get an email telling you that someone has made a post on it. And people make lots of posts on Compass. And they will have emailed the information to you as well as making the Compass post about it.

Exams

The natural enemy of the student. Our students start doing exams in Year 10. Up to then they do tests, but we do indicate to them that exam conditions are a bit different.

The Year 10s usually get the idea, but there is always one student who feels it is a good time to stuff around, make noise and generally annoy everyone. Guess who has already opted to leave school early or go unscored!

We sit them down in a big room, with little individual tables and a supervising teacher. We go through the no talking, no food, no notes routine and let them at it. It is probably a good idea to get your senior students ready for the big exam at the end of Year 12, but I am not convinced that is does a lot of good to run exams in Year 10. Year 11, Semester 2? Yes. But not before. I think it is good that they realise that the major exams of Year 12 are a big deal and should be treated seriously. There is a lot of administrative work associated with Exams. You need to give notice of the date, time and place of SACs (School Assessed coursework) and exams. You need to arrange special conditions for the students that need them. You need to arrange for redemptions for the students who fail. It goes on and on. See your school for local conditions.

<u>Extras</u>

When you have a day off you will need to leave an extra, so that the teacher who takes your class will have something to give the students. These days you can leave extras on Compass or whatever daily organising software your school uses. This means the students can access the lesson plan for the day, and the supervising teacher will only need to deliver a little bit of content and then make sure the students work and behave.

The temptation here is to leave work that is easy for the replacement teacher, like watching a film. That's ok if the film was a part of the unit of work anyway. Try to avoid just leaving films to watch for no reason. Try to make the work worthwhile. This isn't always possible but do try.

If you are taking an extra, you will appreciate it if the regular teacher has left meaningful work. This will keep the students focused. If they know it is just 'busywork' they won't bother too much with it and might start to get unruly.

If you are supervising a class, make your standards clear. If the students know you, your reputation will proceed you and (if it's a good reputation) you won't need to do much to keep the students on task. If they don't know you, make it clear they have work to do, and get them onto it. Feel free to exit any students who are not doing the right thing. This is an extra for you so you are missing out on your preparation time. Don't let them waste your time.

Holidays

You know all of those stories you hear about teachers having fantastic holidays? Well that's only partially true. Yes the holidays are good. But you spend a remarkable amount of YOUR time working on schoolwork.

If you teach a Year 12 class you can almost certainly expect to do some work at home on most weekends. Also, the two week term breaks will be similarly taken up with some school work in preparation for the next term. And the big break at the end of the year is great. And seriously, you won't have to do any work at all for a lot of that break, but you will need to start to prepare for the new school year as January runs out. So yes you get a lot of time away from your school, but you do not really get a lot of time away from schoolwork. Oh and every time you go to a resort or holiday destination, the place will be chock full of kids and harassed parents.

Interruptions to the school year

These are many and varied. Quite apart from the scheduled holidays at the end of each term you have special holidays such as Cup day and King's Birthday. You also have swimming day, athletics day, photo day, and you will find you are missing students toward the end of each term, especially toward the end of term 4. Often you will have more than half of your class away with still a couple of weeks left in term 4. Just be aware of these absences when you are planning your work. You will also have individual kids away with sports teams, camps, excursions, special career days, etc. It really just never ends.

You will also have student free days. At first you think 'Yay! No kids!' but after you have sat through a morning dealing with the Annual Implementation Plan and its impact on pedagogy, you will be wishing you had your normal classes. Look around you. A lot of experienced teachers have mysteriously come down with flu or something on this very day. Strange that. By the way you will notice that is the first time I have used the P word. Pedagogy. What a horrible word. It came swinging into fashion in the early 2000s and everyone was pedagogy this and pedagogy that. It sounded vaguely creepy, but it caught on. Any way, you will have plenty of student free days dedicated to whatever program the education department has spent a fortune on and they will nearly all be a complete waste of time.

The problem derives from the way we have groups of people devising Professional Development programs and then giving them access to public servants. Every new program is going to change the world and quite often they have the germ of a really good idea in them. However, in an effort to maximise profits, the PD Company erects a whole scaffold of padding around the germ of an idea, and makes snappy PowerPoints and booklets for the government to buy. This they then do, and they are obliged to tell principals to get it implemented.

Swimming/Athletics

These are usually held in Term one when the weather is still good. It means it can be baking hot, which is sort of ok for the swimming sports, but not so great for the athletics. Mind you, it isn't so great to be a teacher on a hot day wandering around the pool, wrangling kids and completing whatever job you have been assigned. And if the swimming sports day is cold, it is just a bit better for the poor teachers and the kids don't seem to mind it too much either way.

You will find these sports days are mostly popular with the junior classes. Years 7 and 8 kids mostly get quite involved in it. Year 9 students are pretty disinterested because that's de rigueur with them. Year 10 and 11 students can con their parents that they would be better served spending a day getting stuck into some pretty rigorous study given they are now senior students, and then they go and socialise or play games. Year 12s tend to view the sports days as another 'last' on the school journey so they seem to like to attend.

You will be given a task on the swimming days. Someone has to record times, supervise the various sports, be a starter etc. I was lucky enough to be the only teacher who was into photography when I started teaching, so I was given the job of photographer. This was way back in 2003, and we still used actual film in the cameras, so I was able to leave early to get the photos developed quickly so they were ready to put up on the school noticeboard.

When we moved to digital photography with the rest of the world, I was able to point out that I needed to leave early to download the images onto my laptop and edit them so they could be printed and put up on the school notice board.

Also, as photographer I was able to wander around and take photos as I pleased, which meant being in the shade for good student photos when it got too hot. An added bonus was that I had images of teachers which could be used in the annual end of year staff slide show.

It is amazing how seriously the students take competing in these events. We turned up a few decent athletes who went on to have success in their particular sports. Sadly, the student participation rate has been steadily declining and I'm not sure how long we will be able to justify having an entire day off for swimming and another day off for track and field. I think they are important however, and I guess kids will always like jumping into the pool or running around.

Camps

These can be fantastic, but they are hard work. The key to a good camp is organisation. You have to have lots of activities and it is always a good idea to walk the students as much as is possible in order to tire them out. Of course this means the teachers have to walk an awful lot as well. You can organise some free time for the kids which leaves the teachers time to sit and have a coffee. The only thing you have to really worry about is losing a kid. Which, upon reflection, is a pretty major thing to have to worry about. The only time I lost any kids was on a Year 10 City Survival camp, which I mentioned earlier. We let the kids have an hour of free time and then they were to meet us at the Town Hall in Melbourne.

We broke up from that exact place so the kids would know where it was. When it was time to meet to catch a bus back to our lodgings, we had two kids missing. The others went back on the bus and two of us waited for ages before they eventually turned up. They had gone to the Collingwood Football Club shop which was located, unsurprisingly, in Collingwood which the students thought was just a few minutes away. It wasn't. Bloody Collingwood. The Collingwood Football Club has since moved a lot closer to the Melbourne Town Hall, no doubt as a result of this very incident!

A friend of mine had a dreadful experience on a previous City Survival Camp. A girl went missing. She was missing for some time and the staff had notified police, when she turned up at the prearranged meeting place.

Apparently she had met a guy online, and had arranged to meet him while she was in the city. When he drove up at the place they had agreed on, she thought he looked a lot older than he said he was online and she walked away. I don't think this explanation made my friend feel any better.

The city survival was a good camp. It was originally for Year 10 students, and it worked well. But then the school realised that Year has a lot of events in their year and they dropped the City Survival back to Year 9 where it ran for a few years, before people got a bit wary of travelling around the city with 70 or so Year 9 students for 4 days and nights.

Having said that, I also had a great time in Canberra with a Year 9 camp. It really is an eye opener for our rural students to see what a city is like. Our school used to run camps in Tasmania, and even in Rome and Paris! Our students are not really familiar with the ways of a big city and it is good to see them navigating their way around and seeing, sometimes literally, how other people live.

Sadly, the new agreements and working conditions have just about killed off camps as they are just too expensive to run these days. Back then Teachers worked on the camps often until 1 am for no extra pay. Now they have to get time in lieu at least, and schools just cannot afford to pay the casual relief teachers required to accommodate that. So the students miss out on what can be an important life event. I still remember my Year 11 camp at Inverloch with great fondness.

Public Holidays

These tend to get converted into longer weekends by some students. If the day off is a Monday, you will be missing kids on both the preceding Friday and the following Tuesday. Melbourne Cup day (a Tuesday) became so infamous as a reason to take the Monday off, that most schools just schedule a student free day on the Monday.

<u>Marking</u>

The bane of the English teacher's life. Some other KLAs also have a heavy load of marking. Humanities students get to write a few essays and they write a few short answer questions as well. I mean most faculties do get their students to write material that needs to be assessed, but none have as much as English. Maths just checks the answer and put a tick or a cross. And Art teachers just look at paintings and sculptures from a few different angles. I'm kidding... They don't worry about the different angles. No I'm kidding again. I know all teachers put in the hard yards when it comes to assessing student's work, but I think everyone will agree that the poor old English teachers have to do the most.

There is nothing more disheartening than going home on a Friday evening, with a class full of senior English essays that need to be marked ASAP.

Actually there is something more disheartening than that. It is going back to school with those same essays on Monday morning and you haven't touched a single one. Well at least they have had a little holiday away from school.

Of course, you now have much less time to get the marking done, and, just to really make you feel great, the first question you will be asked when you walk into your senior class will be 'Have you marked our SACs Yet?' This will also be the second, third and fourth question you get until you write on the board 'SAC results due next Friday'.

As Friday approaches you will begin to seriously consider talking a day off to get the SACs marked and you will curse yourself for stating such a short due date. On the following Monday you will point out to the student's the meaning of the word 'due' i.e. 'Expected to arrive imminently' and you will throw a bone by pointing out that you have been really happy with the ones you have read so far.

There will be a reason why you will be happy with the ones you have read so far. You will have started with the best ones first.

My first move when contemplating assessing a class full of essays is to put them in order of expected quality. The ones I think will be best go to the top of the pile, and the ones I know will be poor, go to the bottom. This is actually quite easy to do and you will only need to see one or maybe two examples of a student's writing to know which ones will go where. This is true for any year level.

The reason you do this is twofold;

1. If you start with the good ones, you are less likely to award good grades to an essay that is 'kind of ok' but that reads as magically competent because the first few you read randomly were so crap. If you start with the best, you get a good idea of the standard that your good students are writing at and you can grade them accordingly.

2. As you get more and more tired of reading and assessing essays, they will get shorter and shorter as your weaker students write less and less. The last one or two you have to grade will just be a short paragraph

in total, or maybe the student at the absolute tail end of your imagined quality ladder will have just written their name and the question they were thinking about answering.

There is one drawback to this system and that is that the bulk of the essays will fall in the middle and you will still have to decide where they sit on the scale of things. Remember when you were in that meeting and they were talking about data and there were a whole lot of graphs with boxes and whiskers? Remember the term 'Bell Curve' getting bandied about? This is that. You get a few really good essays, and a few really bad ones. The bulk are in the middle which forms a bell shape on a graph. See you should have listened more rather than just hoping those maths and art people weren't going to ask too many questions.

Marking is an odd process. Everyone has their own way of doing it and you will find that your way of doing it might change from year to year, class to class, and student to student.

If I have a really capable student, I will probably mark hard. I will deduct marks for silly mistakes because they are going to get most of the task right. The essay will be well written because they know the text and they understand the question. Perhaps the only thing they can improve on is their proofreading. I mark these kids hard because I do not want them getting complacent. Obviously I will lavish praise on their efforts to build their confidence, but I want them to strive for improvement as well.

A struggling student who is trying hard might call for a different approach. I do not want to crush them with a lot of negativity so I might turn a bit of a blind eye to a few misdemeanours spelling wise, in order to bolster their confidence with the way they answer the question.

You will get students who will be in tears because they only got 93% on an essay. You will get others who will be quite happy with whatever is a pass mark. Some will ask other teachers to mark their work as well. If you are asked to mark the work of a student who is not in your class, you can by all means agree to do so, but I would ensure that the other teacher knows about it. That will remove any awkwardness. I have never minded other teachers looking at my marking if I am confident I can explain why I gave the grade I did.

I should also mention cross marking here. In Year 12 we are expected to cross mark the students essays. This means that we choose a range of essays from across all of the classes, and all of the English teachers read and mark those essays. I went through this process a few times and generally, we were all within a mark or two of each other. It is pointless getting all argumentative over a mark here and there and so it was a fairly painless process. However, it is a bit tedious having to read and mark more essays from classes other than your own. It has to be done though. Plus it gives you ammunition when a student complains about their grade. You can simply point out that three teachers read it and they can submit it for further reading if they like, but who knows, the grade could go down.

Junior classes are easier to mark but they are just as tedious. Before I started teaching I fancied myself as a bit of a writer. Fiction mostly. It was something I enjoyed and I envisioned myself doing a lot more of in the future. I had a couple of stories published and a play performed. I barely wrote another thing in the next twenty years of teaching until I went part time. I was just too stuffed at the end of the day, and my brain had turned to mush through reading Year 8 creative writing.

<u>Meetings</u> – There are a lot of these.

Staff Meeting - You can expect to have a general staff meeting each week after school. These generally go for about 45 to 50 minutes. If the chair of the meeting starts the meeting by saying 'This shouldn't take too long', then you know you are in for a long one. Also, there will be one person (at least) who will have a string of questions to ask at the end of the meeting. They will probably be from the Art Key Learning

Area (KLA), but they might be from Maths. I don't know why that is the case, but it's the way it seems to be.

These meetings are compulsory and they are agreed to every time the government and the union draw up a new work place agreement. If you have a smart principal, they will use these meetings wisely. If there is something to discuss, they will go with the meeting. If they do not have anything important to announce or to discuss with the whole staff, they might say to just use the time as you see fit.

Other principals however, stick to the letter of the law. If the agreement says they will have a 45 minute meeting once a week, then they will have that meeting even if it means coming up with some nonsense to discuss that could easily be dealt with by email. I have heard Principal class quizzing each other on what the hell they can talk about in an upcoming meeting.

Briefings – These generally occur on Monday morning and are designed to just remind people of events coming up in that week. They are often completed online via Teams or Zoom thanks to the pandemic of 2019/2020. So at least something good came out of it. Usually these meetings take 5 to 10 minutes and cannot go past the first bell of the day so at least there is a limit on the amount of waffle that can go on.

Key Learning Area (KLA) Meetings

How these go is entirely up to your KLA leader. If there is much to discuss, they can go on forever. Of course, if there is a definite aim for the meeting so much the better. English KLA's often spend a few meetings toward the end of the year looking at texts to study the following year. This gives the English staff a wonderful opportunity to suggest a range of books that only one or two will read in the available time, and to then reluctantly stick with the texts that they have been doing for ages, because not enough people have read the suggested texts. Why do you think 'Macbeth' and 'Of Mice and Men' are still studied? I'm just kidding. But I have seen some dodgy books stay on the booklist for years.

KLA meetings also offer staff a wonderful opportunity to whinge about their workload/budgets and other KLA's, although that might have just been my KLA. I'm not really sure what goes on in other KLA meetings. I assume they talk about texts and how they are going to deliver the curriculum. They probably discuss how to improve their results, but for all I know they might all sneak out and laugh about the English KLA staying in the meeting.

Each KLA may also have been given a brief to come up with a response to some sort of procedural nonsensical policy and so their time will be devoted to de-jargoning a departmental missive, so that they can respond to it.

Staff meetings (Special) - every second week you will have to work on whatever program the education Department has nominated as their 'thing' for the year. It won't be sold as that of course. It will be described as a new way of teaching that will enhance the educational outcomes of whoever might be the target. It will have a catchy name and it will be supported by glossy booklets, professionally produced PowerPoint's and it will have funded Professional Development days (see below) attached to it. It will be a waste of time and money and it will basically rehash good teaching practices that all good teachers adhere to anyway. If you have been teaching long enough, this new program will vaguely remind you of a program the department introduced many years, but you wouldn't have paid too much attention back then and you will not be able to categorically accuse the department of rehashing old programs. You see? You should have paid more attention.

Professional Development Days

I'm not going to mince words; these can be nasty. If you are a new teacher you will enter into the spirit of the day and you will arrive with a 'can do' attitude, a folder and pen to take notes, and a willingness to learn new things that will transform your classroom.

If you are a more experienced teacher, your eyes will scan the agenda for the day, and you will mentally mark the tea and lunch breaks.

You will then note the finish time to see if you get let out early and you will feel quite pleased to note that the day is scheduled to finish at 2.30pm. However, your heart will sink when you see that guy from the art department, and that woman from Maths who always ask tons of questions. Your angst will only be slightly relieved by the fact that there are bowls of lollies on each table.

Of course, if you are a really experienced teacher you won't be in attendance, as you have correctly identified the day as a good opportunity to catch up on your marking at home. And you don't even have to write up extras!

Look, there is no sugar coating it, these days are often a complete waste of time. They can be good. I went to one or two good ones that were useful and interesting, but given I've been teaching over twenty years and these things occur at least twice a year, that isn't a good ratio of good and bad. And trust me, if the speaker begins with a getting to know you exercise, or introduces role play...Well it's going to be a long day. These things are renowned time wasters. Honestly, I've lost count of the amount of times a day long PD day has been dedicated to basically saying you need to engage your students and not just talk at them all lesson. And how is this information delivered? By standing in front of the whole staff and talking at us.

Committees

To be fair some of the committees that you will encounter in schools are effective. Obviously that effectiveness is somewhat dependant on who is on the committee and the purpose of the committee.

There will be a curriculum committee that will meet during the year at various times and it will be there to monitor how the curriculum is being implemented and, later in the year, it will look to change how the curriculum *was* being implemented, and whether it needs to be changed or not.

Plus there will be leadership committee meetings that will deal with day to day or week to week issues that arise in the school. How much any of this actually impacts you, the classroom teacher, relies mostly on the issues that your school faces.

There will also be committees that are formed to deal with a single issue. I was on one of these. The government approved a program that encouraged schools to develop a significant policy to improve educational outcomes. By the way, any change, development or response is always designed to 'improve educational outcomes'. It actually becomes a handy little phrase to help you get the things you want;

Teacher – I'd like to spend a few hundred dollars to buy a camera to use in my Media class.

School – How much would they be used? It is a lot of money just for one class of media studies.

Teacher – No, lots of classes could use the camera. English teachers could use it to record oral presentations. Music classes could use it to make music videos to post online. Science teachers could use it to record things blowing up.

School – So you are saying that this camera would improve educational outcomes?

Teacher – Umm. Yeah? I guess.

School – Ok. Not a problem. Buy a couple.

So make a note of that one. Improving educational outcomes.

But I digressed. I did say that I would. The committee I was on was charged with looking at ways of introducing a ban on the use of mobile phones in class. This was before they had become a real problem for schools and I guess it shows that the Principal at the time thought it was going to become a major hassle. We met a few times. We got sent off to an overnight Professional development course and in the end, came up with a really good set of rules on the use of mobile phones at our school. And the rules worked for a while. Our rules were not too different from the rules introduced years later by the department for all schools. I am not saying they stole our rules... But I'm not saying they didn't either.

The point is, committees can be a force for good. Plus it is a good career move to have a few committees scattered throughout your CV.

This Admin chapter is getting big isn't it? Now why do you think that might be?

Honestly, I have worked in a few different workplaces and nowhere is as over administered as the education sector. I understand that you have to have a lot rules but it is amazing how many new rules and regulation have crept in over the last few years.

For instance. A few years ago I was teaching a junior humanities class. We were studying geography. I was a nice sunny day and I knew that just a little way up the road from the school was a point where you could sit next to a small creek, and you could see the way the creek had formed the landscape around it. I had the class walk to the location. There was erosion, there were lots of plants, small animals and insects and generally it was a pleasant way to show students how a waterway impacted the landscape. And we did that just by me deciding it was a good idea and letting the office know we would be out of the school for an hour, in case anyone was looking for me or a student in the class.

If I were to do the same activity now I would go about it in a different manner.

1. Seek permission from the school leadership in writing stating how this would improve educational outcomes (I told you)

2. Prepare permission forms for the students to take home

3. Give the students a few days to get their parents/guardian's permission.

4. Remind the students to get the permission forms signed and returned to me or the office

5. On the planned day of the excursion, phone home to get verbal permission from the one third of the class who did not return their forms

6. Write a lesson to be completed by the few kids who either didn't want to go on the excursion or whose parents did not want them to go on the excursion

7. Phone home to get verbal permission from the parents/guardians of two kids who at first said they didn't want to go, but had now changed their minds

8. Collect the first aid kit

9. Organise the teaching support person who needs to come

10. Remember to submit the possible hazard pro forma that I should have completed at step 1.

<u>Mentor/Mentee</u>

As mentioned elsewhere, if you do not get a mentor appointed to you, go and get one. Choose an experienced teacher who is happy to give up a little bit of time to help you come to terms with teaching. It should ideally be someone in your Key Learning Area, but it does not have to be. Hopefully, all of your KLA colleagues will get around you and support you anyway.

Ask questions. We all go into new jobs being afraid of asking too many questions or being worried our questions are 'dumb'. Just ask them anyway. That's what mentors are for. I think it is also a good idea to get friendly with another teacher who is just a year or two ahead of you. They will remember with more clarity what it was like to be starting out in teaching, and they will be able to advise you on what worked for them in any given situation. Also remember, one day someone is going to ask you to be a mentor. Make sure you give others the support that was given to you.

<u>Parent contact</u>

This is another area that causes some angst. Many teachers just do not like contacting parents. There are reasons for this. As surprising as it may seem, many parents really do not care how their child is progressing at school. I know, it shocked me when I found out too. Fortunately I would say the majority of parents DO indeed care about their children and how they are doing, but a lot don't.

I think parental care breaks down into three categories.

1. They care passionately about the child's education. They attend every parent teacher interview, encourage teachers to contact them at home for whatever reason, and are supportive when their child is not performing well, or is misbehaving.

2. They care about their child's progress but they figure that you will tell them if there is anything they need to know. So you don't hear from them unless you contact them.

3. 'While they are at school, they are YOUR problem. Don't trouble me.'

And yes, I have had parents say that last one out loud. Some parents can be unreasonable in their expectations. They think their child is brilliant when they are middling at best. These can get testy during parent teacher interviews if they think you are at fault in any way. Once again, I was lucky in that my age (45) when I started teaching, made everyone, parents included, think I was an experienced teacher from my first day out. If I said little Marty was not doing the right thing, then Mr. Higgins was right.

These days, most teachers will email home if they have concerns about a student. You can establish a good working relationship with a parent via email and it usually suits both parties, although perhaps not the actual student. When you have met a parent in person, it is easier to remain in contact if the student is not doing the right thing. Again, it is all about establishing a relationship.

I had a colleague who, when confronted with an angry parent either in person or on the phone, would simply advise them to arrange to talk to the principal. She would then hang up, or walk away. The principal does get paid the big bucks for a reason!

If you say to a student that you are going to contact home, make sure you do it. Empty threats are your own worst enemy in classroom management. Similarly, if you tell a parent you will contact them if you have any concerns about a student, do it. The worst thing in the world is when a parent finds out about Marty's deteriorating results in the last few weeks of term when there is nothing that can be done about the problem. The parent will rightly be angry with you, and you will not have done the student any favours by not letting their parent know in a timely fashion.

On parent teacher night it is a good idea to be prepared. These days you will have a list of appointments so you will know who you will be seeing. There are some things you can do to make the whole night a more pleasant and worthwhile experience;

1. Make notes on the students you will be seeing in the order you are listed to see them.

2. Have a sample of their recent work to discuss with the parents/guardians

3. Have notes about their work, their behaviour and make comments about how they are going, and what they could do to improve.

4. Make sure you know the student. Get their name right. Do not confuse Emma Smith with Emma Jones just because they look identical.

5. Be aware of any special needs the student has, or if the parent has pointed out that they are weak in a given area and that they want you to be aware of this weakness.

Parent/teacher nights are usually not stressful as you tend to see the parents of students that you do not really need to see. In other words, the parents who care about their childrens education, who actively support it and encourage their children to do well, will make appointments to hear their teachers tell them that their child is doing well. You then have to spin out this good news for ten minutes. The parents you really need to see do not come to parent teacher interviews. Hmm. I wonder what that could mean? Is there a correlation between good parenting and good students, and bad parenting and weak students? The government might conduct some research into that, but you will never hear the findings of that research.

<u>Reports</u>

Ah ha! Finally, you get your chance to let the parents know all about their little darlings and how they misbehave at school. Well, yes and no. And I should tell you that I put the 'yes' in there just to make you feel better. It's mostly 'no'.

Our school issues 'progress reports' at the end of Terms 1 and 3. These are basically a check box type of report with an entry for Effort, Behaviour, Homework and Preparation and statistics on attendance.

The choices you have for the entries on these reporting areas are Excellent, Very good, Good, Acceptable and Needs Attention.

So if you want to really put the boots into your 'problem' child in Year 8...I mean, if you really want to improve the education outcomes of your least favourite student in Year 8, you can point out that, say in Maths, their effort, behaviour, completion of Homework and preparation all.... Need Attention. There. Strong stuff! That'll learn him.

At the end of each semester the student is issued with a full report. You are about to experience that feeling of Déjà vu. Ah ha. Finally, you get your chance to let the parents know all about their little darlings and how they misbehave at school. Well, yes and no. And I should tell you that I put the 'yes' in there just to make you feel better. It's mostly 'no.' (Did you get that Déjà vu feeling?) At least, this is the case for the junior reports. The senior reports do give a bit more information to parents.

There is a bit more detail in the full semester reports but much of it is not really useful. So what do you get in a junior end of semester report? You get the same checklist of Excellent, Good, Needs Attention that you get in the progress report. You also get an indication of how your child is performing in comparison with the state decreed progression points. This is a statistical tool that was introduced about ten years ago.

It purports to identify where a typical Year 7 student should be placed on a series of levels based upon the information collected through the work they have completed. It is so accurate that every year, when completing reports, you will hear teachers ask, 'So where are Year 8 students meant to be? Is it 8.5 for the middle of the year?' You should have heard the questions when the levels were not tied to year levels.

Anyway, teachers tend to make accurate assessments of what level a child is at, despite having to faff around with all of the curriculum levels.

The reports also give some detail about the work that has been covered, but it is couched in really inoffensive academic language and is probably not much use to anyone.

The senior reports do make comments on how a student has gone with the work. Once again, in order not to offend anyone, the comments tend to be pretty generic.

Here is a selection with translations:

"The class studied 'Station Eleven' by Emily St. Jon Mandel and were expected to understand the concepts being explored in the text. James your essay on the text lacked detail and demonstrated a basic understanding of the concepts being explored. You need to ensure you complete all of the associated worksheets in order to better understand the text.

This is a scathing report. I'm not sure how James survived this. Here is the translation.

The class studied 'Station Eleven' by Emily St. Jon Mandel but James did not understand the novel as he did not read it. His essay was very basic because he did not read the novel, nor did he listen to the novel being read in class. He didn't do any of the work set that would help him understand the novel; this was because he didn't read it.

Teachers litter report comments with lines like,

"Marty needs to ensure he comes to class with the correct equipment." Which means, Marty never brings his books or a pen. Or his laptop.

"Marty has well developed oral communication skills" – Marty never shuts up

"Marty would do well to remember to attend as many classes as possible as he did miss a significant number of classes" – Who is Marty?

Whatever you write, be sure to remember that no matter how much you agonise over the wording and the message you are trying to convey, the student will look to see if they got a C or better based on percentages, as we don't do letter grades anymore. . They will only read the comments if they got worse than say a C or 50%. Then they will point out that the bit that says "you need to ensure you complete all of the worksheets' actually implies that they did complete some of them.

However, one thing you do need to remember is that you really shouldn't be too honest about a student's abilities. You cannot make personal statements or get sarcastic. If you want to do that you need to write a book about teaching teenagers.

<u>Smoking/Vaping</u>

Weirdly, this has not been a major problem at our school. When smoking was popular we had groups of about ten students who regularly smoked. When I was on yard duty I used to start to walk toward them so they all had to put their cigarettes out. I would then walk away, but turn around and approach them again just after they had lit up again.

I have heard stories of kids vaping at school. I even heard of a student vaping in class! I just think it is all too expensive for a lot of students. I know one enterprising student who was selling cigarettes to $2 each. That's probably cheap these days.

I have heard about students using drugs but again, I don't have any first-hand knowledge of this. Once when I was a Year 11 Co ordinator, I had a student say that he had purchased a pill from a Year 12 student. I took the pill to the local chemist. It was a vitamin pill. I think I am lucky in that I have only taught in a rural school. Yes I know that rural areas have drug problems, but it just was not a huge problem for us. I hope it stays that way.

<u>Student Representative Council</u>

I knew our school needed a reintroduced SRC when I heard some students complaining about the cost of food at the canteen. I told them they should tell the SRC and get them to do something about it. They asked me what an SRC was.

And so our Student Representative Council was born again. These groups can be quite powerful if you get the right students involved in it, and you have a supportive Principal. You do need students who are willing to commit to attend occasional meetings and they have to be willing to push for change in areas that need changing.

Our SRC was very successful. It comprised the school captains and various form captains. They came up with some great ideas and after a while, I didn't need to guide them too much and I ended up just advising them about the best way to approach an issue.

Sadly, the SRC slowly died through a lack of impetus as the original keen members started to focus on study and there was no one to replace them. Perhaps it is something that needs reintroduction every few years to keep it fresh.

Getting involved in the SRC does look good on your CV if you apply for an ongoing position at the school, or for a job at another school. It shows an interest in the student welfare and that you are prepared to give of your time to further the students and schools interests. It also looks good on the students CV when they start applying for jobs. Employers like people who give of themselves like that.

Student Teachers /Pre service Teachers

If you are asked to supervise a student teacher do so. It is a great way to reflect on your own teaching whilst helping a new prospective teacher to learn the ropes. If you are new to teaching yourself, you will be in a unique position to be able to offer recent advice about your own teaching.

Watching a student teacher and making notes about what they are doing right and wrong will help you to remember to do these right things in your own class. It is really interesting to watch your class being taught by another person. You know all the little signs to look for and you will get a good feel for how the class operates when you are out the front.

I used to provide student teachers with a few pages of running commentary on the class. It took the form of brief observations like;

Good start. Settled them quickly.

When a student arrives late ask them where they have been.

James had his cap on. Get him to remove it. Emma was chewing gum.

When you ask for hands up, scan the room. Marty had his hand up three times and you didn't notice him. He gave up after that and lost interest.

Don't talk until they are quiet.

Don't let students wander around.

When you are chatting one on one to a student, you must scan the room. James punched Marty as he walked by him on the way to the bin.

He then slipped Alan's pencil case into the bin. That was the cause of the disturbance.

Stuff like that.

Student teachers are a bit like students doing an Oral presentation. Some are nervous and you can tell they know the content, but they have trouble overcoming their nerves at times. Others are really confident, know their stuff, and are able to convey the information to the class effectively. Actually, most pre service teachers know their subject really well. If they didn't it would be a worry. I don't imagine anyone would feel comfortable going in front of a group of teenagers without being confident that they knew what they were talking about. A few really struggle with classroom management and that is understandable. It is not a skill that is needed in many other jobs and it is the one that causes the most angst for new teachers. Some of course, are naturals. They are the lucky ones that just seem to have the confidence and ability to control a class. It is a skill that can be learned, otherwise there would be little use for this book. And it is something that will improve with experience. By the same token I have met teachers who claim that they have 'lost their Mojo' and they just don't seem to be able to get on top of a tricky class. Other teachers freak out at the start of each year (and the start of each term in some cases) and don't settle until they are a week or two into teaching.

If you are asked to supervise a pre service teacher, be kind and fair, but be honest. You are not doing anyone any favours by saying they can control a class when they cannot.

<u>Theories of Teaching</u>

There are lots of theories of teaching and honestly, I feel that there is probably something of value in all of them. I just don't think that any one theory covers all eventualities. Yes some students will benefit from a very laid back, 'minimum rules' approach, but that same approach would be disastrous for other students. Montessori Schools are not for everyone. The Berry Street model is not for everyone.

If your own feelings about the benefits of one school of teaching are strong then you should probably seek to teach at one of the schools that advocates that particularly method of teaching. Or alternatively, you could introduce aspects of that method into the way you teach at your present school.

My own feelings are that you need to provide aspects of different methods in your class. This is called differentiated teaching and it is expected that you will be doing this anyway. It is a very tricky thing to do. Your class is going to have a range of abilities. As mentioned elsewhere there will be a majority who will fall into the middle of your bell curve of abilities. The really strong kids will be able to operate with minimum supervision, but you will need to provide them with extension work, or more challenging material. Your students at the other end of the bell curve will need easier work and you cannot just make it shorter. You need to tailor it for their needs. You can imagine how much extra work this generates. Next year someone will release some studies that show that a blanket approach is more suitable as it encourages the weaker students to strive for excellence and the stronger students will provide role models. It won't work either.

The differentiated model is probably the method that best approximates what teachers would normally do in any class anyway. Teachers naturally provide work that suits a given student's abilities.

All of the programs that will be introduced in your teaching career will just tinker at the edges of useful teaching models.

An old Assistant Principal once told me that the Victorian Department of Education and Learning made two major bad decisions;

1. Making the leaving age 17. Governments have been raising the leaving age for years as it lowers the unemployment rate each time you do it. You then end up with loads of 17 year olds who do not want to be at school, but have to stay there as they can't get a job. They can be disruptive and have a bad impact on the success of other students.

2. Allowing Professional Development companies to have access to the Department in order to sell them educational programs. This means that when they develop a program, complete with texts, PowerPoints and day long in house programs, they sell it to the government. The government is then obliged to force the schools to introduce the program to justify the cost. Then the schools have to hold whole day PD to get the staff on board. These one day PDs are usually ok for an hour, and then padded out to make up the day. A waste of time for everyone.

The Gradual Release Model

Released in a fanfare of Professional Development announcements, the Gradual Release Model was unleashed with textbooks for all, PD days galore and guest speakers.

It boils down to this

Teacher Responsibility Student Responsibility

I do it Focused Instruction

We do it together Guided Instruction

You do it together Collaborative Learning

You do it alone Independent Learning

This was presented in a double pyramid graphic. I imagine the development of this program went something like this;

Developer 1 – Ok we have this idea that the teacher shows the kids how to do something. What would happen after that?

Developer 2 – Perhaps they would gradually tell them what happens in the whole process.

Developer 1 – Gradual release! We can call it that! And this first step can be focused Instruction. What would happen next?

Developer 2 – They'd do it together?

Developer 1 – So the teacher would guide the student. Guided Instruction. We can have this as the student's role or responsibility

Developer 2 – So then the student would do it alone? We could call that independent Learning

Developer 1 – Nice one. Independent learning. I like it. Can we expand this to fill a whole day PD?

Developer 2 – It needs something else. "I do it. WE do it....YOU GUYS DO IT TOGETHER! "And then you do it alone!"

Developer 1 – You know what that is? That's Collaborative Learning that's what that is. That's a good hour or two in the PD. (High Fives all round)

The Peer Review Model

This one was hated by staff. Basically, it meant that a group of senior teachers came to your class, made notes and then left after about ten minutes. We were told not to worry as this was meant to be a reassuring practice that would help us to develop better classroom strategies. It freaked people out. It was really intense, distracting and annoying. Like most other introduced 'models' the program was thrown together by some Professional Development company, sold to the Department, with bolted on PD, and then forced upon the schools and individual teachers.

I'm not saying the model is faulty, but the way it was implemented was very dodgy. Schools often do not have the resources to complete such a program successfully.

I know that, at the time, I would not have liked having to give up my free periods to go and watch another class. I'd do it occasionally, but too often would have been too much of an ask. I didn't get any feedback from the visitors to my class and they only would have had very limited material to comment upon anyway.

Having said that, I would suggest asking a trusted colleague to visit your class every so often would be a good idea. You can get them to critique the way you start the class and how you operate. You can get into bad habits and if you get a friend to critique you, it will be a useful and painless exercise. If you want you could pair up with someone who is a bit ahead of you career wise. You could also offer to repay the favour by looking in on one of their classes and offering your thoughts. It is all good professional development. I haven't heard anyone refer to the Peer Review Model for some time so I assume it has gone the way that these things tend to go. It probably cost a lot of money too.

FISO 2.0

Get that hip, up to date title! FISO stands for Framework for Improving Student Outcomes. Now, as I have previously stated, it would seem to me that 'improving student outcomes' has pretty much been the core business of any school for the last couple of hundred years. Actually many see the birth of 'schools' in about 3000BC in Egypt and Mesopotamia. I imagine Plato and Aristotle had meetings with various people where they discussed how they could improve students' outcomes. Ok they might not have had breakout sessions and Team meetings, and I doubt that they had a critical friend (ask someone who was teaching in around 2010) but who knows?

This new FISO, (mark 2.0) obviously hits the nail on the head educationally. It is a framework. It has five core elements. This is from the department website:

The FISO 2.0 sets out 5 core elements that together realise the goals of excellence and equity through developing the learning and wellbeing of every Victorian student.

When integrated, these elements build a positive environment through strong relationships that enables all students to become:
- *happy, healthy, and resilient*
- *successful lifelong learners*
- *active, informed members of just and sustainable communities.*

Let's unpack this shall we?

"The FISO 2.0 sets out 5 core elements that together realise the goals of excellence and equity through developing the learning and wellbeing of every Victorian student."

I do not think that the goals of excellence and equity can be said to have been realised until AFTER the implementation of the FISO.

And not every student is going to have their learning and wellbeing developed.

The "When integrated" bit is probably an 'out' for the department or the company that came up with this one. If student outcomes are not improved, well clearly the staff involved did not 'integrate' it properly. Look let's face it, this is all fluff. The trouble with these programs is that you have to wade through reams of guff like this, choc full of buzz words and jargon, to uncover the germ of a good idea. The department would have spent a mint on this. The rest of the quoted piece is just the same tired old clichéd phraseology that gets trotted out with every new program.

The five core elements will really rock your world. Ready? Ok, hope you are sitting down.

The five core elements are; Leadership, Teaching and Learning, Assessment, Engagement and Support and Resources. I mean, wow. Ok, not quite out of left field. I imagine they had a bit of a headache coming up with 5 core elements. Teaching and Learning, Assessment, and Engagement pretty much write themselves.

I bet they regretted pairing Teaching and Learning as there are two elements you could have had right there. I reckon someone suggested 'Support' but it was probably felt to be a bit thin on its own so they tacked on 'Resources'. This still left them one short as you can't have a professional program with only four core elements. It doesn't look neat. I daresay someone said 'Well someone needs to lead all of this' and they settled on 'Leadership' as the fifth element. And then they put it at the start of the list to make it seem more important.

The FISO 2.0 is a large, impressive document. And it is growing.

It is an ongoing program. It has the usual steps, such as gathering and assessing data, examining current processes and practices, identifying and planning actions and Implementing and monitoring impact.

So I guess it is time to disregard the data that has been collected over the past ten or so years at the instigation of other programs. Schools will probably be instructed to form committees to examine current practices, and another committee will be created to identify and plan actions and then a task force will be formed to implement and monitor the impact of FISO 2.0

Except that, by the time all of this takes place, another program will have been introduced to do pretty much the same things under a new name. Although, to be fair, the use of the name FISO 2.0 might indicate that they will aim for a FISO 2.5 or even a FISO 3.0. At least that saves them coming up with a new name. After that they will declare that FISO has been embedded into each school's curriculum, whatever that means, and they will happily seek out some new shiny thing to introduce.

I can pretty much guarantee that the only time 90% of teachers will even think about FISO 2.0 is as they are walking, reluctantly, to another staff meeting on this subject. To think it will have any lasting impact on a student's educational outcomes or wellbeing is laudable, but unlikely. If you want to make a dramatic shift in the educational outcomes and well-being of students, you are going to have to improve teacher training, run a campaign to improve parental skills, decrease the workloads of teachers and, in an ideal world, pay them more.

Do not hold your breath.

<u>Visitors to the school</u>

You will occasionally get visitors to the school. You might see someone wandering around the school and it is not only polite to ask them if they need help, but you are obliged to do so. Remember you have a whole load of kids here and this stranger could be anyone. If you are not sure about them, escort them to the office.

Just tell them that it is a legal requirement that all visitors sign in at the office. If they refuse for whatever reason, call the office and inform them of the situation, and get someone from leadership out to help you. There have been cases where estranged parents have come to schools to pick up children they are not meant to pick up. You need to be careful in these situations. If the person is at the school for a valid reason, they will be happy to sign in and follow the rules.

I like it when we have guest speakers at the school. It gives the students a different perspective and a new voice to listen to. The only thing to watch out for are speakers who do not have an idea about how teenagers operate. We had an Indonesian puppeteer visit the school once, and the show just went on and on and on. He thought that, because he found the topic fascinating, everyone else would have the same level of interest. Limit the time a speaker can speak for before a break.

Other than that, your job it to make sure the students are respectful, and well behaved. Mostly they are, and they appreciate the change from their teacher droning on and on. As you can see, there has been many ways in which administrative details have influenced the way we teach. There are forms for everything. And there is a bewildering array of acronyms as well. It will take you some time to get to know all of the administrative requirements, however, the good thing is that a lot f it does not really matter when it comes to the teaching part of the job.

Staff

Over time, schools become weird places to work. Each year you lose one whole year level of students, and then you acquire a whole new level of new students at the start of the next year.

Each year you also have about 5 or six changes to the staff. Sometimes more, but rarely less. Sometimes the staff leaving will be key, important staff, and other times they might be influential and well liked. Sometimes both! If a school loses a lot of teachers at the end of a year, you can be sure that there is something wrong at that school. It might be a personality thing, or it might be a student cohort problem. Whatever, large groups of teachers bailing out of one school happens for a reason. Be wary.

You will have very close working relationships with a handful of staff, and your mentor. You will make friends with a certain group of people. You will also be a part of a larger group in your KLA. You will then have another grouping based on your staff room. Then there will be staff that you are friends with and with whom you socialise with out of school.

Then there will be staff who you don't really know well, but who you always seem to see in the corridors and in the photocopy room due to a quirk of the timetable that sees you both free at that time. And, there will be one staff member that you are not sure is even on the staff. You will see him or her occasionally and you will nod pleasantly to them as you pass. You will only see this person maybe once every few weeks. You will wonder who the hell they are, and they will be wondering the same thing about you.

Assistant Principals

After you have been teaching for a few years, you may decide that you really like the administrative side of things (it does happen trust me) and you might begin to see yourself following a career path.

If this is the case you will have put your hand up to be on tons of committees, completed tons of PD and perhaps even enrolled in Departmental programs designed to promote leadership skills in the education sector (in order to improve Educational Outcomes of course). You will now be viewed as a possible future AP. There will be a tension among the staff that are on this path as they strive to get the next AP job in the school. Some of course will apply for AP positions in other schools. Anyway, it will be good if you can specialize in an area of administration like Data management, or Teaching strategies or even child psychology. Some schools have a couple of AP's and they tend to focus on one area of teaching that the school can point to in its Annual Implementation Plan. (See the entry in Admin). At the moment our school has three AP's. No one knows why.

<u>Canteen staff</u>

The canteen staff are just people trying to do a difficult job and they don't need teachers strutting around like they are better than everyone. Don't treat canteen staff badly. And don't push into the line just because you are a teacher. Most canteens like their customers to pre order their lunch as this makes things easier for them. Also keep canteen staff happy. They control the food. Be good to them.

<u>Careers staff</u>

Strangely unrecognised in Victorian education for many years, the careers department is very important to the educational success of a school. I always wish we had a careers officer when I was at school. It would have taken a lot of the guesswork out of employment prospects for many students, However, my current school is fortunate to have a couple of people who are good at the job and who care about the students. My feelings about them are not influenced in any way by the fact that our Head Careers person always buys me Kit Kats for Christmas.

<u>Cleaners</u>

You only really notice the cleaners when they aren't there. Be good to cleaners. They have a crappy job to do. You know how hard it is cleaning up after ONE teenager? These people have to deal with mess left by hundreds of teenagers! Do the right thing by them and make kids pick up any rubbish they drop in the classroom, or around the school. Talk to the cleaners. I can't believe I have to say this, but I do know that some people think cleaners are somehow below them on some made up social importance scale. A clean school helps you with your classroom management. Recall a time when you walked into a really untidy, messy classroom. Remember how the kids were 'off' that day? Untidiness can do that.

<u>Daily Organiser</u>

The Daily organiser is the person who allocates extras and in lieu classes (classes that you have to take because your own class has been cancelled for whatever reason). Now, knowing that, can you believe that there are actually people who treat the Daily Organiser badly?

Just imagine upsetting the one person who could give you an awful Year 9 class in the last period of a Friday. Why would you do it? I have found the best thing to do with the daily organiser is trust that they will be fair. Always say yes to extras. You are only meant to get a limited amount of extras per fortnight and per year. If the Daily Org asks if you would mind doing an 'extra' extra, just say yes. This means you will probably get a 'good' class for that 'extra' extra and the Daily Org will look after you regarding extras in future. It is just common sense.

<u>Dress code for teachers</u>

I know some teachers who would love to have a uniform for teachers. The general consensus is that neat casual will serve quite well for teachers, but that leaves a lot of room for improvisation. One man's 'Neat Casual' is another man's weekend grot clothes, but I suppose that depends on the men. I used to wear jeans, a decent shirt and plain shoes all of the time and I was considered something of a snazzy dresser at our school. I have known people to wear suits. I have also seen a few people rock up in track pants and tee shirts. Your leadership group will advise you if they feel that you are letting the side down.

I think the only contentious aspect of women's clothing was the fact that open toed shoes are a no-no. It is a OH&S thing apparently.

Oh and given the fact you are dealing with teenaged boys it is a good idea to wear modest clothing. I did know a female teacher who wore a low cut top quite often. Even another female teacher said that she felt mesmerised by the sight. So you know, use your common sense.

<u>Educational Support Staff</u>

I have mentioned these before but they are worth discussing in more detail. If you get a good ES staff member in your room you are laughing. You have another adult in the room, so you have another set of eyes. The better ones help the class run smoothly as well as helping individual students complete their work. Usually they will have one assigned student to help, but often they end up helping a few kids.

Sometimes, the assigned student will not want the Educational Support person sitting with them. They do not like the fact that they need 'special' help in a class and will try to minimise it. Savvy ES staff work around this by helping everyone.

I have known ES staff who go on to become teachers but there are surprisingly few of them. I think the hours and conditions of being an ES staffer suit some people, plus they have seen what tons of correction and lesson planning can do to a person.

<u>Groundsman</u>

I do not know why but groundsmen (or groundswomen) often are fairly eccentric characters. They always seem pretty laid back and casual about everything. They always love a chat. They can be quite useful apart from their regular gig of maintaining the school grounds. Often they will take a troubled kid under their wing and let them work with them, instead of being punished by sitting with the Principal class. Plus they can do stuff like instruct students on trees and plants, report any students hiding around the school in weird places. I once got our old

Groundsman (Hi Parko!) to come in and talk to the students about the jobs he had done over the years. I also got him to make a time capsule for me. (See Year 7)

IT Staff

I will give you the tip; never bad mouth IT staff. The reputation follows you. If you criticise the IT staff at one school, and then move to another school...They know. It's weird. It's like they have some sort of magical connection.

Fortunately I have generally had a good relationship with IT staff simply because I treat them in the same manner as I treat office staff or the Daily Organiser. Anyone who could make your life hell, you need to treat well. Our IT staff have always been happy to give me advice about computing in general and they were mostly really good at conducting little seminars whenever a new program was introduced by the school or by the department. I never saw them get frustrated with computer illiterates who just didn't get what they were meant to do with a program. I mean, I'm sure they did get frustrated, they just didn't show it.

These days, good IT staff are essential to the smooth running of a school. You only need to turn up on day one of any term to see this demonstrated.

You will see a queue of people (teachers and students) waiting to have their laptops updated, or their passwords changed, or printers added to their laptops etc. Honestly, the IT department at any school could bring the whole school to a standstill if they wished to do so.

KLA's (Key Learning Areas)

Each of the KLA staff groupings will have a certain flavour to them.

English Teachers – Generally really good looking, smart and good teachers. The collective noun for a group of English teachers is a 'Delight' as in "I just walked by a delight of English teachers. My god those people are clever." Feel free to approach a Delight and say Hi. We love improving the day of other teachers. Teaching is a 'vibe' thing for English teachers. They love food.

Maths – The natural enemy of the English Teacher. Where 'close enough is good enough' for the English teacher, Maths people like specifics. The collective noun for maths teachers is a 'problem' of maths teachers. They often tease English teachers by confusing them with talk about pi.

Science – A sort of poor man's Maths teacher. They get a bit sick of being typecast as crazy professor types who like to blow things up, but, to be honest, they really do like to blow things up. Don't let Science teachers get onto your schools 'buildings and maintenance' committee.

Humanities – The KLA that knows its place. Warm and fuzzy types who would secretly like to take the students out to hug trees. Strangely however, they love units on the study of War.

Art – Weirdly, these people who are all meant to be creative types, adore administration. They always ask questions in meetings that mean the meetings go overtime. The Art KLA includes Music, Food, Woodwork, textiles etc.

PE – There is a lot of joking about the mental acuity of PE teachers. On reflection that is stupid as PE teachers tend to be fit, fast and strong. I think they're great!

Library Staff

The library has lost a little of its importance recently with the rise of laptops and digital books, but it is still an important place in the school. You can break up the routine of weekly classes by having a class in the library. I know I have said that you need to stick to routines in your class but I also said it is good to break that routine every so often. So there you go, you can't trust anything I say. Bloody Teachers.

The library is a good place to do some research using those quaint old fashioned things called books. I used to begin my Year 11 Macbeth unit with a book activity in the library. I would arrange the tables so they formed one big workspace, and then I would pile all of the books that had any information about Shakespeare in the centre.

There were old copies of the plays, reference books, biographies etc. The students formed groups and had to find the answers to about 20 questions about Shakespeare and his works.

Most of the questions were just general knowledge questions and some dealt with the play Macbeth itself. The students always loved this activity. It probably appealed to that sensory aspect of learning and they just liked the feel of the books. You do not get that same feeling with a screen.

Our library staff over the years have been fantastic at encouraging kids to read, and providing a safe place at lunchtime for some of those odd kids who always seem to coalesce around the library and IT spaces. The only time I had anything bad to say about the library staff was at the end of the year when they gave you a list of the books that you still had out. If you had returned them all you got a chocolate frog. Now I know I returned them all, but I couldn't prove it and this 'fictional list' was held against me every year. I never did get a frog.

Office staff

Why anyone would treat office staff badly is a mystery to me. These people are very powerful. Always be nice to office staff. If they do not like you, your life can be a misery. Plus they are always nice. (See what I did there?)

Principals

Of course, this is the last step on the ladder. A good one is worth their weight in gold which I suppose means you should hope they stack on a bit of weight. A bad one can ruin a school. I have been lucky enough with the Principals I have worked with as they have generally been good.

It isn't a job for the faint hearted. You need exceptional people skills. You also need exceptional administrative skills, organisational skills and you need to be a bit of an all-rounder. Some Principals teach a class or two, but some just do not have the time. I had one Prin (You might as well get used to calling them 'Prin' as everyone will) who had the timetabler put her in for one class early in the year. Unfortunately the Prin had to attend to so many other matters that they constantly left extras all the time which wasn't fair to the class, or to the other teachers who had to do the extras. They soon changed the timetable.

A good Principal will protect their staff from some of the more useless pronouncements emanating from the Department of Education, whilst a poor one will try to implement EVERYTHING that comes out of the Department of Education. Trust me; the second type has been known to bring schools to the brink of extinction.

Principals are often called upon to defuse clashes between students, between staff and students and between staff. They have to be able to deal with union issues, employment issues, emotional issues, privacy issues and they will often be called upon to deal with staff and student personal issues. They will face legal issues, health and safety issues, budget issues and the fact that the staffroom has run out of coffee. Lots of issues!

It takes a special sort to do it well.

The Social Staffroom Fridge

Don't go near it and certainly do not store food in it. I don't know about other schools, but we have a social staffroom where people go to get hot water and milk for their coffee if they do not have a fridge and kettle in their own staffroom. This means that all sorts of people use the fridge, but no one actually cleans it up. There will be stuff in there from ten years ago probably. The only reason the milk is usable is that staff need coffee. If you really want to freak staff out, hide the coffee. Anyway, they do chuck out the milk after it has developed the consistency of yogurt. And the sink in the staffroom is even worse.

Welfare Staff

I did this for a year. I learned more about why difficult kids behave the way they do in this one year than I have in all of my years teaching.

Some of our kids live horrendous lives. You would not believe what some of our students have to put up with in their day to day lives. Drugs, violence, starvation, poverty and bullying. It's awful. The welfare staff usually do a wonderful job in assisting students cope with things in their school life and their home life. Sure, some kids play the system and get out of class by 'going to welfare' needlessly, but for the ones who really need it, Welfare can be the difference between a successful education and failed one.

Year Level Coordinators

I have mentioned YLCs before but I thought I had better go into a bit more detail about them. Each Year level has its own dedicated coordinator. Sometimes there will be two YLCs and sometimes there will be an assistant YLC. Also, at our school, there is another position that oversees the junior and senior coordinators. Being a YLC has its positives and negatives.

Positives – You develop a much closer relationship with the students in your Year level. You get to know them in depth. I should also add here that you will get to know some of them in far more depth than you wished had been the case. There is no getting around the fact that you are going to spend most of your time dealing with kids who cause problems.

You will also spend a lot of time with kids who are unable to deal with the problems that they have caused, or that others have caused for them. Actually I seem to have strayed into negative territory here.

You will get to reward kids who do the right thing. It's actually quite a powerful position. The students tend to see YLCs as being in control of their lives somewhat, as they are the ones who can bring incredible rewards for good behaviour. (Some Co ords organise excursions/special lunches/canteen vouchers etc) However, YLCs can also call down the wrath of parents and guardians. Whilst teachers are expected to call home themselves to solve problems with students, if this is not the solution it should be, the call can be handballed up the chain to the Year Level Coordinator. Cast your mind back to when you were at school. Imagine having to go home knowing that the Year Level Coordinator has called your Mum or Dad, or worse, both, during the day. Not good. I seem to have strayed back into the negative side of things again.

You get a little bit of time allowance, so you are at least out of a class.

You possibly get a small office with just a few other coordinators in it.

Negatives – You develop a much closer relationship with the students in your year level. Otherwise, see above positives.

You possibly get a small office with just a few other coordinators in it. Well it all depends on the other people!

You

Let's talk about you. I'm going to just assume that you know why you are teaching and that you plan to stay in the profession for a little while at least. How can you make it easier on yourself? That probably sounds a bit ominous I suppose. Why should you be looking for ways to 'make it easy on yourself'? What the hell have you got yourself into? I have said that I have worked in a few different industries and places, and I can honestly say that teaching has been the hardest of them all. It is rewarding. It is rewarding in many ways. But it is also the toughest job I have had. It is difficult mentally and it can be difficult physically. I know that if you have been in teaching for a little while you already know that it isn't just a case of having tons of holidays, leaving at 3 pm and cruising through the school year reusing old lessons and generally having a great time.

Before I started teaching I used to do a bit of fiction writing. Nothing too amazing, but I had a couple of stories published and I thought I would one day get a novel up and published. From the day I started teaching I barely wrote a word of fiction. When was I going to do it? I was too tired or busy marking during the week and on weekends

I needed to do other stuff and plan for the next week. Ok it wasn't like that every day of my teaching life, but teaching exhausted me enough to impact other areas of my life. Non English subject teachers should probably skip the next bit.

If you are an English Teacher, you have big classes. I've routinely had classes of 24 students every year. And marking essays takes time. In senior classes you can have 23 or so major essays to mark regularly, and that's not counting practice essays and other assignments. Plus you have a classroom with many kids who have not chosen the subject and do not particularly like it. English teachers get a real dodgy deal.

Ok you teachers of other subjects can come back in now.

So how are you going to cope? You need to be fit. I know that sounds weird but honestly, if you are unfit or a bit poorly, teaching will really find you out. It is stressful, and it will test you. Get fit and maintain a good level of fitness.

Look after your mental health. You will notice teachers saying they are going to have a mental health day. Everyone does it, often once a term. You just take a day off to relieve the pressure. Don't take a day off to catch up on correction as that defeats the purpose. Take a sickie. Go to the beach. Relax.

There is a tendency for new staff to try to make themselves indispensable so that the school will renew their one year contract. Or they might just feel the need to present themselves as competent and willing to work. This is admirable, but do not let it go too far. Many new teachers burn themselves out by taking on too many extra jobs. Do not do this. The more you take on the more you will be expected to take on. I guess it is like the old saying; If you want something done, ask a busy person. "Oh Anita is organised and a hard worker. Let's ask her to get the school camp organised.' And all of a sudden poor old Anita has a lot more work to do. Remember, you have more than enough work to do just as a classroom teacher.

Do not put your hand up for more. I tend to be a people pleaser myself and I have agreed to do extra work that I didn't really want to do, and I ended up getting very resentful. The best advice I ever got was that it is always easier to say 'no' and change your mind, than to start off with 'yes'. Learn to say NO. Whoever is doing the asking will probably just shrug and say 'fair enough' and then go and ask someone else. Teachers are generally decent people, but you will get some who will want to manipulate others for whatever gain, just as in the general population. Often the person asking you to do something extra, has themselves been asked to complete the task and they are just looking to handball it to someone else.

Eat well. If you can, go somewhere other than your desk to have lunch. I just read that in France, it is compulsory to move away from your desk to eat your lunch. Not just in teaching, but in all walks of life. It is a good rule. My school used to have a one hour lunch break in the middle of the day. Teachers would flock to the social staff room to eat, chat, do the quiz etc. It was a very popular place, and it encouraged camaraderie amongst the staff. Then we had a major overhaul of the school timetable and we ended up with two short lunches of 25 minutes each. People stopped going to the social staffroom and ate their lunch at their desk. Not only did they not get a mental break from teaching, but staff morale plummeted. The staff had been notable for being cohesive and supportive. Slowly this was eroded as the staff were divided up into smaller staffrooms.

So eat with a bunch of other staff. Of course, if you have a really good smaller staffroom, you can socialise there if you want, but I think the idea of getting up and moving away from your desk is useful. In my last staffroom, we tended to turn our backs on our desks and sat around a couple of tables in the centre of the room. That way we could chat and eat, and we were not at our desks. That was a very good staffroom.

If you are in a toxic staffroom, you need to request a change. Look it happens. Sometimes a staffroom can just be a bad mix of people, or people have stayed a long time and have become jaded and cynical (I mean more cynical than the average teacher). These people seem to delight in constantly discussing how bad students are, how useless parents are and how annoying teaching is, but they never seem to make a concerted effort to get out of teaching. They just like whingeing about it. This can be contagious. See your principal and get out. Tell them it will improve the educational outcomes for your classes.

Have a life outside of teaching. Get a hobby that takes you out of your house, and your comfort zone. It does not have to be nude bungee jumping ... although if that's your thing, go for it. Just have something that gives you joy. You will need it at times to take your mind off teaching. Oh and I would encourage you to make it a physical hobby. Your brain is going to need a break as well so make it something you can get into physically.

Occasionally, plan a week of classes that give you some relief. Develop a major piece of work that is going to mean the class is busy researching and putting some sort of major assignment together. Oral presentations are good for this. If you can get all of your classes doing it at around the same time, it can provide a great break for you. You won't have to plan lessons so much and you can spend some time wandering around the class making connections with kids. Or, stagger the projects so you have some normal classes and one or two easier ones. Get creative with your planning. Often these days every person teaching the same class will be doing the same things at the same time, so collaborate with your colleagues and organise the term's work appropriately.

Learn to switch off. I guess this is related to the previous point. I used to work for a department of the Federal Public service that dealt with classified material. We were not allowed to take work home obviously, and this extended to taking work home mentally. They really encouraged you to totally switch off from work mode as you exited the building. That was a very good lesson that I had to relearn for teaching.

I have had many sleepless nights worrying about teaching. It is crazy what goes through your head at 2am. Anyway, try to leave work at work, and I know you will have to do correction or lesson planning out of hours, but do try to minimise that when possible.

Go for a walk around the school when you have a free and it is a nice day. Actually, if it's really nice you can take a class for a walk around the school. This is one of the nice things about teaching. You are master of your domain to an extent. You used to be able to do a lot more creative stuff with classes, but now everyone is following strict curricula and there just isn't time. I remember when we studied the book 'Holes' by Louis Sachar in Year 9. It is about a place where convicted boys go to learn how to be good. They do this by digging holes in the scorching sun. There are a few plot threads going on, but the point is, my Year 9s decided that digging holes like that would be fun. I liaised with our groundsman (see relevant entry) and asked him if there was anywhere he wanted dug up. He gave me a few shovels and off we went. We sat around while groups of kids dug holes. They didn't last long, as I knew they wouldn't, and at the end of the lesson they had a better understanding of what the boys in the novel were facing. You probably could not do the same thing today without filling in a risk assessment form and getting permission from home. The point is you still have a modicum of control and you should use that to give yourself some reasonably easy classes. You don't want to be a teacher who just stands at the front of the class droning on and on all the time.

In a similar manner, we were reading 'Hatchet' by Gary Paulsen in Year 8. A great book that boys love. A young boy is involved in a light plane crash in the Canadian wilderness. He has a hatchet and that is all. Before the plane crashes the boy has to fly it a bit. The pilot, who has a heart attack, had previously shown him how the controls work. Anyway I demonstrated with a paper plane. That evolved into a whole lesson making paper planes, having paper plane competitions and the students learnt lots about physics, paper planes and, I guess origami. Educational outcomes all round!

While we are talking about you and how you cope with the day to day stresses of teaching, I should mention that there are two schools of thought about travelling to and from school. I live about 25 minutes brisk walk from the school I teach at, so obviously I drive to and from work every day. It takes me about 7 minutes to drive there as long as I don't catch the lights and/or a train at the railway crossing. God I hate that. It is fantastic being so close to work. I can nip home when I have forgotten something which happens sometimes. So I can get home really quickly if I want to do so.

However, I do miss 'coming down' from a tough day with some music on the way home. When I did teaching rounds, one of my schools was a good 45 minutes away, and I would listen to music all the way home and all the bad stuff would be out of my system when I got home. I am not saying you need to move if you live close to your school, but it might be a good idea to do that shopping on the way home or, if you can get home quickly, do something that releases stress. Chop wood or dig in the garden or something like that. Or I suppose you could just drive around aimlessly until the stress has gone away. I know this sounds like a small point to make but trust me, you will need to decompress some days and often there will not be anyone around that you can vent with.

But then again just taking 7 minutes to get to work is a big plus too. So yeah, there are pro and con aspects to the whole deal.

Students

Year levels.

What follows in a rundown on each year level. I should emphasise that these are just my experiences, thoughts and reactions and the experiences of other teachers may be wildly different. I doubt that it will be THAT different, especially with Year 9 kids, but I thought I should put that qualifier before you go taking my word about any year level as the gospel truth. Besides which, every year level is different. Next year's year 7 cohort will be different to this year's kids. Sometimes they can be wildly different. This is why you get teachers saying 'Oh wow this year's Year sevens are crazy.' So do remember that these comments should be taken as just my experiences. There are a lot of different factors at work here.

I should also point out that there will be individuals in each year level who will shock you, surprise you, please you, annoy you and generally act in a way that is totally outside of your experience with that particular child. In other words, they are all individuals.

<u>Year 7</u>

You will first encounter the new Year 7 cohort when they attend orientation day at your school. I mean, our school does this and I just assume that most schools do the same thing. They might not. Anyway, my school has a pretty wide catchment area when it comes to students, so we have a lot of feeder Primary Schools. The main one is right next door and the bulk of our students come from there.

Anyway, you will see groups of Primary school kids wandering around your school, doing activities and having a great old time. Your current year seven kids will gawk at them and they will be very pleased that they aren't the 'little' kids anymore and they will have someone below them on the pecking order.

The new students will range from the incredibly shy to the outrageously confident. You will look at kids and think 'He/she is going to be trouble". You know how sometimes you just know? Probably politically incorrect but that is the way it goes. If you have a class during orientation day it is good to let them know that you are excited for them and how it is all going to be wonderful when they start Secondary school the following year. I mean, let's not ruin their dreams just yet. Remember these kids mostly think that finally school is going to be the wonderful and fantastic place they have been dreaming off when the promise of primary school was shown to be an empty husk. No not really, but they will be excited and rightly so. Be exited with them.

When the first day of the new school year rolls around you will have bunches of nervous kids wandering around and most will settle once they find their friends from primary school. You will also have bunches of nervous parents as well. I have only seen tears twice on the first day of school (that's not counting the teachers) and both were new Year 7 kids who didn't really know anyone. A decent Year level coordinator will quickly pair them up with a nice group of kids.

The school gets lots of information about the new cohort of students. Most of this relates to behavioural problems that some of them have, and of course, having a feeder school next door means we have lots of siblings coming into our school to join their older brothers and sisters. If there is a lonely new student they can often be paired up with the little sister of brother of an existing student who is known to be nice.

The whole school will probably have an assembly and it is generally full of buzz and excitement. The first day of school is a great day, until about the second or third hour by which time it has just settled into the routine you know. Anyway, everyone else will go off to their form groups and the Year 7s will all stay behind.

Let's assume you have a Year 7 form group. You will go off to one side and the coordinator will say a few words and then he or she will read out the various form groups and point them to their allotted form teacher. Once you have got your lot in a bunch, you can lead them off to your form room. They won't have any classes scheduled for the start of the day so you should have a fair bit of time to introduce yourself. I try to avoid too much information on this first day, but you do want to get them used to a routine as soon as possible.

Make sure they know the name of their form room and where it is located. Our rooms are based on directions so they need to know which way is North, South, East and West. Then allocate lockers. You can pre do this if your coordinator has given you a list of lockers for your form group. Then you can just go down the list alphabetically to allocate lockers. Some kids will whinge that they have got a bottom locker and all you can do is say they can ask for a top one next year. This effectively handballs the problem to next year's Year 8 teacher, but they will have forgotten all about it by then. You can give them a spiel about keeping their lockers tidy and indicate that there will be locker inspections. When you get back to the room tell them that if they have any problems, they can talk to you or any other teacher. You really do just want them to feel comfortable interacting with you. Remember we are all about building rapport and you need to do that quickly with your form group. I am assuming you will also be teaching them in at least one subject. Our timetable always gives a Year 7 form group teachers a normal class with that group as well. However, there have been occasions when someone will just have a group for form assembly. Timetable clashes do occur and it isn't a perfect system. You can show them the locations of their rooms for the rest of the day. This will make them feel a bit more confident about the whole thing.

Year sevens are a bit of mixed bag.

This sounds like a dumb to say really as any group of approximately 24 kids is going to be a mixed bag, but they do seem to be more so in class groupings. You will have the quiet girls, the princesses, the sporty types, the joker boys, the moody ones, the happy go lucky ones and the studious ones, plus all of the other variations that exist. You will also have a mix of abilities and it is a good idea to get a handle on just what their abilities are pretty early on.

I know this sounds terribly boring but you can get them to write an introductory letter about themselves. Stress that you want it to be hand written and be sure to have paper and pens handy for the students who have neither.

Of course, you will need to give them an example and this is mine;

Hi,

My name is Mr. Higgins. I am really pleased I got to be your form group teacher and your English teacher. Welcome to Trafalgar High School! This is a great place. I have taught here for over twenty years so it must be good.

You are probably wondering what I am like and I know I am wondering what YOU are like so that's why I am writing this introductory letter to you, and it is also why I am going to get you to write a letter about yourself to me!

I like sport. I like to watch football and cricket. I used to play both of these ages ago. I am married and I live here in town so you will probably have seen me wandering around the shops. I like to garden and we have a garden at home that we are pretty proud of. I particularly like to grow things I can eat, because I love food. We have a bit vegie patch, and lots of fruit trees. We also have bees, so we get honey from them sometimes. I have only been stung twice.

I also teach Year 9, 10 and 12 English and Year 12 Media. If you ever need to speak to me you can find me in the staff room down in the W building, near the library.

I am looking forward to our year together.

Mr. Higgins

That's it. I would hand out a copy of that and read it aloud to them. As you can see it is pretty basic. I have kept it very conversational and informal. I have used words that they will be familiar with and generally I have made it user friendly.

I am not an expert of Year 7 capabilities. I have no academic qualifications to guide me on how to frame material for a Year 7 mind. I am just using what I know works. Some people might claim we should be using challenging vocabulary and teaching the students the basics of formal essay writing, but I think that's nonsense at this stage. I just want an indication of what their skills are like and some basic information about them. I have deliberately included things like hobbies and interests as I want them to tell me what they are interested in. I want to know what they like to do on the weekend. And I will read their own little introductory letters and I will make notes on spelling and sentence construction and anything else I feel is useful, but I will especially take note of any interests that they might have. Remember building a rapport with students? It starts here. On day one.

So far on this first day I will have made sure I spoke to them in a quiet reassuring voice. I will have sounded confident and I will have sounded positive. I will have provided a calming presence as I gave them information and I would have constantly reminded them that this is just their first day. They will not get into trouble for being late, of getting lost, or anything like that.

Now I also have some indication of where they are at educationally. I know it isn't much but you will be able to tall a lot about a student's academic abilities through a short writing exercise. Some Students will not write much at all. You will find yourself suggesting topics they could write about. (Tell me about your pets, siblings, football side, parents, house, friends etc. You are the expert on you!)

Some, particularly weak students, will feign boredom with the task. It isn't necessarily that they can't be bothered with the task, it could be because they cannot complete the task. Maybe they cannot write? Maybe they have not understood your instructions? Try to get them to write something. Be prepared to be shocked at how poor some of their handwriting will be. Be prepared for how little some actually write. Be prepared for some to write pages of material.

You don't have to give this little task back to the students. In fact I tell them it is just for me and my use. I don't actually mark it, but I read each one and I make notes about writing skills, sentence construction and spelling. Just basic stuff to give me an idea on what needs to be the main focus.

The only other thing I would worry about on the first day of classes would be an introduction to school and class rules. Again, emphasise that they are not going to get into trouble if they forget a rule at this early stage.

After about two or three weeks I would start to enforce the rules about being on time, with the correct materials. Our school allows the new Year 7 classes to pack up five minutes early so they can get to the locker and then get to the bus or train. But that is just in the last class of the day.

I like to walk the students around the school, pointing out places that Year 7 students traditionally have made their own. I also point out all of the toilets, the senior areas and good places to hang out. It is also a good idea to introduce the idea of Homework to your students. Homework seems to be falling out of favour these days, but let's face it, if a student isn't going to get the work done in class time they are going to need to do homework. It is a good habit for students to get into early as it gets harder to develop good work habits as you get older...Trust me on this one.

Anyway, just point out that they should aim to do just a little bit of homework regularly each night, or each night that they have had your class. When we had 75 minute classes, we only saw the students three times a week, so I would say just do English homework on those three nights. And it does not have to be a lot of homework. Even if they just start with 15 minutes of homework, and it could just be reading sometimes, then that is a good start. You can increase it to 20 minutes later.

I give homework based on that week's spelling test words. Just basic stuff like finding a definition or putting the words into a sentence. But you can also give them skill based worksheets. There are some text books that are good for this sort of thing. Check with your KLA Leader or the library.

General behaviour.

I haven't had a lot of serious behavioural problems with year sevens. Early on, they can be very needy, and clingy which is only natural. You will get the odd naughty boy and naughty girl, but there are not too many of these. It can be disconcerting however, when someone that small can think they are able to intimidate you. I am lucky in that I was always considered 'old' (remember I started teaching in my forties) and was therefore also considered experienced even in my first year of teaching. Kids know experienced teachers don't put up with too much usually. I am also very tall, so I do tower over them and I use that to my advantage when I need to.

I have had a couple of students who were just bad. They lost their temper, threw chairs around and stuff like that. There isn't much you can do when a kid totally loses it like that. In that situation however, you do need to protect the other students, and the individual who is chucking the wobbly. If you cannot get a duty teacher to get the student out, then you need to try and get the student outside of the class. If that is impossible to do verbally, then you can get the rest of the students out of the classroom.

Remember they probably know that student X can go off and they have probably had to deal with this sort of crap before. Send them to a neighbouring class temporarily so that teacher can keep an eye on them. Do not leave the offending student alone, and do not send him anywhere unsupervised. My best advice is, once you have safeguarded your class, sit down near the student and talk quietly and calmly to them. Yelling at them is not going to do anything but inflame the situation. Besides, they are probably yelled at by the parents and are inured to it, so it won't have much impact anyway.

Talk quietly and softly. They will want to hear what you are saying and hopefully they will stop yelling or screaming or whatever they are doing. Just keep up a monologue.

"I can see you are really, really upset and I am ready to help you whenever you like. If you want to come here and sit down we can talk about it and maybe we can find a solution to the problem. Look there is only a bit of time until lunch and we both want to have something to eat so how about you tell me what the problem is?...No you don't have to yell I'm just right here. Do you want a drink of water? We can go get a drink if you want. I get that you don't want to do that work we were doing but I was just wondering if there was something else upsetting you." That sort of thing. Just keep it up until they respond in a reasonably conversational tone and then you can keep the dialogue going. If the duty teacher turns up you can ask them to keep an eye on your class if you are making progress. If you are not making progress you can handball the problem to the leadership team or the coordinator. They will probably have a good idea on how to handle the student. But, if you do handball it, make sure you make contact with the student before the next class. Just ask if they are ok, and did they get that problem sorted.

If they open up to you, then take their concerns seriously. If it is out of your league you can tell them that you think this is a serious problem and that perhaps we (note the 'we') should go and see Welfare and see if they can sort out 'our' problem. Just that little idea of owning their problem once they share it with you is useful in building rapport. And we all know how important rapport is don't we?

You may find that this student will request to speak to you if they have similar problems and that should make you feel very proud because you have won their respect. By the same token, some children just need an awful lot of time and help and you cannot dedicate yourself to solving severe issues that need a professional in the field. Some students will soak up a lot of your time and you need to remember that you have other students who also need your time. It is a balancing act.

You might also encounter some silly bullying behaviours. Some of this might be carried over from issues in primary school. Some of it will simply be because they are still finding where they belong in the form group and in the year level. You need to keep an eye out for low level bullying and nip it in the bud. Do not let this sort of thing grow. At the first sign of it you can give them a talk (Use your 'disappointed' voice) but do not name names. Just point out that bullying is not tolerated in your classroom, in this school, nor in any workplace. If they don't like someone just ignore them.

The most annoying aspect of inter class clashes is the tiresome "She's looking at me" claim that seems rife at times. I mean, it is so stupid that you don't really want to dignify it, but it can persist and develop into something worse. After the usual, 'Well don't look at her' instruction has failed I often invite the' lookee' to move seats so they cannot see the 'looker'.

After the statement that they have done nothing wrong so they shouldn't have to move, I then just repeat the 'well don't look in her direction' line and just plough on with the class.

If it raises its head again I point out we need to sort this out at lunchtime if it is a major problem. That generally solves the problem.

Having year sevens can be like herding cats but it can also be fun, and you should enjoy it when possible.

I like to get Year 7 classes to write a letter to their future self and put it in a Time Capsule. I don't do this until later in the year when they have settled into friendship groups and have an idea about how the school works. I supply each with a sheet of paper and give them a few ideas. They need to remember that the person reading this will be them, in Year 12. They can write about their hopes and dreams, family, pets.

They can mention favourite music and films. It is open slather really. Try to get them to write as much as possible, as the more they write, the more they will get out of it in Year 12.

I have had students include twenty cents for themselves, as well as small gifts that are important to them, but space is a consideration so nothing too big. They put their letter in an envelope with their home address on it, in case they leave the school before Year 12 (many do) and they seal it, and I put it into the time capsule. This is a length of PVC pipe, with a glued lid on one end and a screw lid on the other. I then 'bury' it in the bottom drawer of my school desk. It always goes down well in Year 12 when they read their letters.

Your school and in particular, your KLA will have copious material on what texts to study in Year 7 and what the curriculum will look like, so I am not going to go into that here.

I do however want to point out one idea that I think is a good one regarding the teaching of Year 7.

Many schools have gotten into the habit of allocating Year 7 classes to new teachers. They do this because it is thought that year sevens present the least amount of trouble, and that the new teacher will be able to cope with lower levels of this behaviour than would be the case if you threw them into a Year 9 class. But then they give them a Year 9 class anyway as 'the pain needs to be shared around'. My friend Cynthia believes that the best, and most experienced teachers should be taking Year 7 classes. This way, they get used to set procedures and ways of behaving early in their school life. They also get set in good work habits and how they organise, or should organise, their books and locker. I think this has got a lot of merit. Good, experienced teachers can do the heavy lifting that will improve the students' work habits for the rest of their school life. It is actually a stunningly simple and good idea. The fact that it hasn't been adopted wholesale across all schools is worrying. Maybe a lot of schools do it? I haven't heard of it being widespread practice, but I know it doesn't happen in our school

A related idea is that experienced teachers should also get the difficult classes. You know the ones; that Year 9 class with six or seven real difficult kids in it, or that Year 8 class that gives everyone a rough time. The problem with this is that you are dealing with experienced teachers. These people know the approaches to use to avoid a dud class. They know that getting jobs that come with a time allowance will lessen their chances of getting awful classes. Some teachers just refuse to teach too many bad classes. I am a great fan of 'sharing the pain' and think everyone should take a shot for the team.

There will be some teachers who will put their hand up for tricky classes. The pay off with these kids is that not many of them do much work so there isn't too much correction to do. But that's not the reason why teachers volunteer to take them. Oh no. No they do it because they feel that all students have a right to decent education and by hell they will get it.

Yeah I'm sure that's the reason. It's probably a bit of both to be honest. I have taken VCAL classes knowing that it won't involve too much correction, and I have put my hand up for 'Foundation' English in Year 9 with the idea that I might be able to get them to improve their skills.

Oh and at some stage you will be asked to conduct a vote for the form captain. At our school we have a Year 7 camp which involves lots of team building activities and gives the students a good chance to get to know who are the most responsible, trustworthy kids that might make a good form captain, and then they all go and vote for the 'coolest' kids

.

Year 8

During Terms 3 and 4, your Year Sevens turn into Year Eights. For some it is a gradual process and for others it is overnight. Anyway, when you acquire your new Year 8 class you will notice that they have grown considerably since last year. If you taught Year 7 in the previous year, you are probably expecting much the same if you have been given the same class, however, there are always lots of changes from the previous year. The year level coordinators chop and change classes around to try to ameliorate the mix in each class. However, even if this did not occur, the kids would have changed a bit personality wise anyway.

Year 8 kids can be fun. No, honestly, they can. They still have some of the little kid about them, and they haven't as yet turned into full on teens. Well most of them haven't.

We will assume that you have got a Year 8 form group this time. Like the Year Sevens, you will start off the year in a whole school assembly. The students will be welcomed back and the Principal will make a speech. Then you and all the other Year 8 form group teachers, and students, will go to a Year Level assembly. This year's Year 8 coordinator will give them a spiel about being organised, getting to class on time, and general administrative things they need to know about.

If you get a Year 8 form group you can cruise through the initial form group meeting simply because these kids know the drill. I would use the first form group meeting just to reiterate class rules, punctuality and school rules they may have forgotten over the holidays. Also, if there have been any major policy changes in the school, you should mention them now if they impact the students. In the first couple of student free days at the very start of the year you will have been made aware of and new school policy changes that you would need to tell the students. New phone policy, out of bounds areas, that sort of thing. You do not need to explain any new teaching programs that the education department has put in place because these will not impact the students in any way at all.

After the students have whinged a bit, you can then make sure everyone has a timetable and you can remind them to be on time for class. If there are any new students, you can appoint a nice student to be their buddy until they get settled. Let the students know where your staffroom is located in case they need you for anything, remind them not to be late for class, and then you can either send them on their way if it is just a prolonged form group meeting. Generally this first day set of three meetings (whole school assembly, Year level assembly, form group meeting) takes up all of period 1, so the kids will go to recess or whatever little break you have, and then to period two. Hopefully you reminded them not to be late.

Obviously your first Year 8 class of the year will start late because not all of the class will arrive on time. You can use this time in a fruitful manner by writing some class rules on the board, perhaps setting up whatever you want to do in terms of table positioning, etc.

As with the Year 7 classes, I am not going to spend a lot of time recommending texts to study or what to teach your students.

Once again your KLA will have worked out a good timeline for the teaching of your Year 8 class so that they are all doing the same topics at roughly the same times. So you will be able to collaborate a lot with your colleagues and you will be able to get sound advice about how to teach the material. I would just like to add that for English classes, Year 8 kids love 'Hatchet' by Gary Paulsen. I know I've mentioned this before but I thought I'd throw in a reminder. There is a series of books but the first one is the best one. There is also a film version which, despite being very dated and cheap, is quite good. Your boys especially will love it and it is quite short. And there is a ton of support material knocking around online even though I have said to be wary of online lesson plans. Anyway that's my only 'English teacher' moment. Sorry about that other KLAs.

As with the Year 7 classes, you should seek to implement a set routine for each class depending on your KLA curriculum timeline. You will need to stick to this routine for a few weeks and then you will be able to judge when the students can handle a change to the routine. I have mentioned that our junior English classes have a set amount of reading time at the start of each period and that is a good settling activity.

As with all of the year levels, you will get to know your kids really well by the end of the year. Some moreso than others. It is odd, but there will always be one or two that you just do not get to know at all. I don't know if it is because they are overly shy, or if you just don't 'click' with them. It is odd.

I did mention that you will get an idea when your Year 7 students begin to turn into Year 8 students. I'm not sure that is the case with the change from Year 8 to Year 9. It is more an attitudinal thing. A vibe...An almost supernatural, eldritch phenomenon.

Year 9

Traditionally, Year 9 is viewed as a difficult year. The students are still finding their way academically and socially. They will want to try and test boundaries in all aspects of their life, and obviously this includes school. I have had some fantastic Year 9 classes and I have had some bloody awful ones. I guess they aren't that different from Years 8 and 10 after all.

One word comes to mind when discussing Year 9 and that word is disorganised. Actually quite a few words come to mind but I am trying to keep this upbeat so let's just stick with disorganised. They really have trouble getting their act together and are oblivious to the mayhem they cause as they go. Many teachers dread getting a Year 9 class, but I think the same rules apply when teaching Year 9 as they do any other year level. You just need a rapport. Oh and a cattle prod. Nah I'm just kidding about the cattle prod. We aren't actually allowed to hurt the students. In these modern times you really need to control that urge to hurt students. No seriously, you do.

However, there is no getting around it, Year 9 can be challenging. Of course you will get your fair share of compliant, polite students who work hard and want to do well. But most of your attention will be taken up with huge boys who have no idea of their own strength and who think it is uproariously funny to be physical with smaller students. You will get those eye rolling, princess types and you will really have to try hard not to laugh when they do the eye roll. I mean, it is funny and so clichéd, but laughing only seems to make them angrier. Trust me, I know.

The year will start with the usual whole school assembly, Year level assembly and then form assembly. Your Year 9 class will view form assembly with some disdain. By the way, I am just assuming that you will have form assemblies. You might not! Our school does and it is really just a chance to mark the roll and let students know about anything special happening that day. Most kids get a bit lackadaisical about it and toward the end of the year, many will just skip it.

I think routine is probably more important in Year 9 than Year 8. Years 9s are a bit like Year 7 in this regard. They are both really finding their way and the more routine in their lives the better. I tend to just stick to my timelines for a lot longer with Year 9 and just allow the usual breaks of routine that come with school sports and other interruptions. Once again, however, that is just me.

If you are an English teacher you will want to find a really engaging text to study. I still haven't found one that the nines have universally loved. On the other hand I have discovered a few that they absolutely and universally hated. Your KLA colleagues will have chosen texts and units of work for your school.

I think you have to be a bit more determined to enforce the completion of homework with these kids. I really advise that if you set a due date for a piece of work, you need to stick to it. Remember that these people are disorganised and you will have to constantly remind them, and when they do not submit a piece of work, set it for homework. If it still isn't submitted, organise some lunchtime detentions until it is completed. Do this early and you won't have to do it again until they forget to complete the next piece of work, which might not be long at all now I come to think about it.

Year 9 tend to want to see how far they can go with bending the rules. Actually, some of them are more interested in seeing what happens when they break the rules rather than just bend them. It is as if they think the rules will make an interesting noise when they break them. My school has a long, large room just near the Year 9 locker area, that is a great shortcut to the canteen. Good planning guys!

Anyway, all students are banned from using that long room as a thoroughfare, but they always still do.

My staffroom was near this long room and the Year Nines were the bane of our life. Every recess and lunchtime you had an ongoing battle with Year Nine kids openly defying your instruction to turn around and go back around the building. It got very tiresome. You had to challenge them of course, but we all pretended we didn't see them sometimes, just to avoid a confrontation. I know it was wrong of me to do that and I am very sorry.

We used to take the Year Nines on the City Survival Camp. Some people wondered who the actual survival part of the camp applied to, the kids, the staff or the city. However, being country kids they were suitably daunted by the traffic, people, business and pace of the city. Well for at least the first ten minutes anyway. Then their confidence kicked in and off they went.

I mentioned it in the camps entry, but you really do need to walk Year 9 kids a lot on camps. You have to burn that energy off so that they will actually get some sleep that night. You know, actually shut up before 2am and go to sleep. Many is the long night I have spent walking the corridors of the hostel we were staying at, knocking on doors and telling kids to go to sleep. Great times.

Speaking of which, Year nine students can really talk. They do not stop talking. I hate to sound sexist but the girls especially are a concern in this area. It isn't necessarily that they talk more, but they have a higher pitched voice and it just cuts through. It cuts through more if they are laughing about what they are talking about. And they say 'like' a lot. I know everyone does, but like...wow. These people are champion likers.

Like all other students, Year Nines are really into fairness. The worst thing you can do is be unfair. When you are having a verbal stoush with a Year 9 student you must be honest and fair.

If they can see you are being fair, it makes them look foolish if they are responding in an unfair manner. During the negotiations you will probably get the student's friends weighing in to the argument. Again if you are being fair, they will point this out to their friend. "C'mon mate. He's being fair. Just finish the work.' However, if you are being unfair, they will join in the argument and prosecute the unfair argument.

And speaking of being fair, always give kids choices. "You can move here and do some work, or you can be exited and do some work. Entirely your choice." This gives you some wriggle room. I like to negotiate with students rather than just impose punishments. If you haggle, the students feel like they have some degree of control over what is going to happen.

My favourite bargain was over word limits for essays.

Student - "What is the word limit? How much are we meant to write?"

Me - "I'd like at least 1,000 words,"

Student - (incredulously) A Thousand?!

Me - Not enough?

Student - (Even more incredulously) No! Too much! I can't write a thousand words!

Me - Can you write 500 words?

Student - (sensing a win) Yeah easy. I can do 500, no problem.

Me - Well do that twice.

Nines are capricious. You will have a couple of good classes and you will think you have found the answer to Year Nine. You will tell anyone who will listen that you think you have finally worked out your Year 9 class. Then the next class you have with them will be bloody awful and you will be back to square one. I think the best approach is to expect the unexpected.

Year Nines can be bewildering. You should have picked that up already. You will have kids in class who are pains, but you will see them on their own in the schoolyard and they will be polite and sensible. They probably couldn't explain the change themselves. It is a strange thing.

I have had students approach me in the street and apologise for being such pains in Year 9. My stock answer is 'Everyone is a pain in Year 9'. Ok they aren't all a pain but a few can be. I have also had students who were just awful in Year 9 and were fantastic in Year 10. Hormones I guess.

I have asked Year Nines about their thoughts on school and they have been reasonable, sensible and critical of their own efforts in class. They know they aren't working hard, and they know they should be more disciplined in their studies and you never know, they probably will be when they get to Year 10. Or year 11. Or year 12. It will happen.

The same students have offered sensible comments on their attitudes to school. They complain about the state of the toilets, the inability of some teachers to explain things well. They appreciate the fact that the topics and texts they study are more challenging. They appreciate the way that the difficulty level of the work tends to go up year to year. However, they would appreciate more tailored work for students. They know that some of them do not cope with the work they are given and they bemoan the fact that they all have to do mostly the same work. They are pleased that they can access TAFE course in Year 9 but they say that there should be more hands on learning for students who learn better that way. These are all thoughts of actual Year 9 students. As I said, changeable.

Some schools have a totally separate Year 9 campus. This was mooted for my school for a while, but I think the funding just wasn't there, however it does demonstrate that most schools acknowledge the challenges that come with Year 9. I wonder if those Year 9 students who are packed off to a different campus realise that they are being segregated. I am not sure they would view that as fair.

Swearing – This seems endemic in Year 9. I don't know why swearing should be more prevalent but it might all a part of the pushing boundaries thing I discussed earlier. All you can do is really enforce the advice I gave under swearing. Most students will comply with your request to cut the swearing if you explain that you find it offensive.

Again my recommendation is to approach it in a low key manner. If you make a song and dance about it, they will just get encouraged to swear more as it has elicited an entertaining response. A quite reasonable rebuke is boring to them. I often make a student swearing a topic of one of my famous one to one 'chats' which the students find even more boring. Boredom can be useful as a punishment. It is a killer in the delivery of content in class, but it can pay dividends when trying to manage a single student and their behaviour.

Technology – Many people argue that students are really computer savvy these days. Some of them probably are, but what they are really good at is playing games. Year 9 students, in my experience, have the greatest problems using technology in class in a responsible manner. They are naturally inquisitive as they are learning about the world. This means they are looking for content. However, they are also looking for entertainment and they are prone to distraction in much the same way that the Pacific Ocean is prone to waves. Year 9 is the distracted year, which fits in with the disorganised idea, so anything that has lots of content, is entertaining and distracting is just made for the Year 9 mind. So technology, the internet and your average Year 9 mind work like a perpetual distraction machine.

Childish behaviour. Remember that you are dealing with children. These students don't all develop in the same manner at the same speed. You know how some Year sevens can be really annoying with their silly noises that they think are really funny? Well it can continue through to Year 9. It only fades away as the individual student realises that their peers are looking at them as if they are crazy. Once that happens, the dumb voices and stupid noises cease. Other childish behaviour may persist. See manufacturer for details. In other words, talk to the parents. Don't tell them that their child is immature, but do say that their child occasionally behaves in an immature manner. It is a big difference.

It is the same as telling a student not to behave stupidly. You don't say 'You are stupid', you say 'You are behaving in an inappropriate manner.' If they want clarification, you can say 'You are a Year 9 student, yet you are not behaving like one.' Actually they are behaving exactly like a Year 9 student, but you want to discourage the behaviour, not encourage it,

I guess the upshot of all of this is that Nines can be painful and they can be really good fun. After a few years you will encounter ex-students in the street. They invariably apologise for their behaviour in Year 9 and you will be surprised that they have somehow magically changed into a human.

Year 10

Very much like Year 9 but with added hormones. Like the previous year there is a lot going on with Year 10 students and there is a lot going on around them as well. Our school had to take a camp away from Year 10 as we just couldn't fit it into the busy calendar.

For a start there is almost always romance in the air, so there is that to unsettle them. Their social life and life outside of school is just starting to really take off, and there is a lot for them to contend with, which often calls for a change in their priorities. I'm afraid actual school work can slip down the list of things to do until it rests somewhere between taking the dog for a walk and cleaning up their room. Yes it can go that low.

There are still a lot of very immature individuals in Year 10, but some have begun to mature into young adults. This has given rise to one of the policy problem areas in schools.

Some years ago the Department, in its wisdom, decided to introduce early entrance for Year 10 students into VCE classes. On the surface this was ok, but only if they limited the early entrance to students who were capable of actually doing the VCE work. Sadly they didn't.

It was a free for all and resulted in some very immature students who were basically Year 9 level and below, sitting in classes with proper Year 11 students and generally ruining the class. I had VCE Media and ended up with a mix of students who were mad keen to study media, and another group who didn't have the faintest idea what they were doing there apart from the fact that they had heard you watch movies in Media. I refused to allow early access in my Media classes after that. The Assistant Principal at the time assured me that if I didn't allow early access, the next year's Media class would not have enough students to run. I stood my ground and I said I would rather no Media class, than a compromised one. This early access scheme only applied to elective subjects.

It was really a dumb idea and its implications were not thought through. Later they changed the application of early access so that only students who demonstrated some aptitude were allowed to access the program.

In English, (You knew I was going to talk about English didn't you?) we had some great texts in Year 10. Steinbeck's 'Of Mice and Men' was always a favourite, as it was short, entertaining, and had a great filmed version. We also started the mainstream students on Shakespeare with 'Romeo and Juliet' which didn't have quite the engagement levels of the Steinbeck novel. Our accelerated classes (see separate entry) had already been introduced to Shakespeare and they always seemed to like it, but the mainstream classes have always thrown up a bit of resistance. You can engage them of course and a decent English teacher will find ways to get the kids into the Bard. Yes it can be done. Generally, the students appreciated the more challenging texts and general work.

We also had a curriculum plan which treated the Year 10 mainstream classes in much the same way as the VCE classes. The students would study the same areas as their VCE counterparts but with easier texts. Again, the thinking is that this will help them become used to the type of work that they will face in VCE.

Unfortunately the same thinking has permeated down through to Year 7 where even our junior classes study Language Analysis. This has not had the desired effect. It was thought that constant exposure to the same sort of ideas through the year levels would help them to understand the more complex ideas encountered in Year 12. What happened was that they were actually sick and tired of these topics by the time they reached VCE, as opposed to being comfortable and familiar with them.

Our tens also have a Deb Ball. No I am not writing this in 1957. When I went to school Deb Balls did not exist and I was very surprised when I found out about it in my first year of teaching. The Deb ball occurs usually in Term 3. It has changed a few times. When I say it occurs in Term 3, I mean to indicate that the actual night is in Term 3, but the preparation begins around February with gown purchases, shoe shopping etc. It is a big deal socially for the kids and they love it, but I know a few teachers regard it as detrimental and a social throwback to the bad old days.

Many students will also be starting part time jobs and this can impact their studies. They view getting paid for work as taking a priority over schoolwork and they throw themselves into as many hours as they can get. We have had to contact home and request that parents limit the amount of work some students do as it just gets ridiculous. Don't get me wrong, it is good to see these kids working and showing some initiative, but it is a concern when it starts to impact their results.

As I indicated earlier, we treat the tens like VCE in some ways and this includes exams. They have half year exams, which are pretty light on really, and end of year exams. It doesn't really impact on their grade but it does give them an idea about what exams look like I guess. For the poor old English teacher it does mean an awful lot of marking right at the end of the year.

If you teach Year 11 and Year 10 it can be overwhelming. Again, I am not sure that treating Year 10 students like VCE students is a good idea. Yes, exposing them to exam conditions can be beneficial, but it means that by the time they get to sit exams that really do make a difference to their lives, they have become blasé about them.

After the exams, our students go to work experience placements. We used to hold these halfway through the year, but it is better to do it at the end of the year. The students are a bit more mature and local businesses can do with the help before Christmas. It has always been a really positive experience for our students. For many years we had a timetable where teachers would go and visit students at their work placement. That was always good fun. Nowadays it is just the careers staff who do the visiting, so lucky them I suppose. However, I have been told that many Year 10 students do not take up the offer of Work Experience. Many of them have part time jobs and now that we have it at the end of the year, many students would rather begin their holidays early.

Years 9 and 10 were always lumped in together as Middle school. So you had 7 and 8 as juniors, 9 and 10 as middle, and 11 and 12 as senior. The divide is down the centre now. 7, 8 and 9 are juniors, and 10, 11 and 12 are seniors.

I think we have lost something by treating the tens as seniors. Yes many are ready for it but a lot are not and they do get discouraged and daunted by the work they have to do. To alleviate this somewhat we have what used to be called the Victorian Certificate of Applied Learning (VCAL) which kicks in at year 10 with junior VCAL.

It is now called the VCE Vocational Major. It provides a place for students who favour hands on learning and who see themselves as being suited to trades and apprenticeships. This program works well but you do have to fight the 'We are VCAL and we don't do schoolwork' mentality that does creep in. Did I say creep in? It barges in. It throws the doors off its hinges and storms into the room like a mad thing. I taught VCAL for a while and all of the VCAL teachers had to really try to get rid of the stigma that VCAL students carried in the school, and that they indeed perpetuated with their 'no work' attitude.

The other thing about Year 10 students is just how much they grow. Year 10 boys can be huge. This can be a bit daunting for a teacher of smaller stature, but you do need to remember that for all of their life so far, they have taken direction from adults. Well most of them have anyway. Clearly some have not had any direction from their parents and that will have spilled over into their school life. You will be surprised how easily you are able to get a huge Year 10 boy to follow your directions. Most of the time. And when I say 'most of the time' I clearly mean some of the time. No, not really. They generally do what is asked of them.

A friend of mine who is also a teacher has a theory about more senior students. She thinks that if an individual or even a group of students are being totally cooperative and compliant, they are playing with your mind. I think there is possibly some truth to this. Organising Year 7s is like herding cats. To organise Year 8 you first need them to be in the right place at the right time. Year Nines can be organised, but not without a lot of eye rolling and muttering. Year Tens will seem to be agreeing with you furiously, but sometimes you will find yourself wondering why, if they agreed to a certain course of action, are we now doing something else entirely?

Generally I think most teachers like teaching Year 10. They are a bit more mature than the junior classes and you do not have (as much) of the silly immature behaviour that you get with sevens and eights particularly.

Most of them have a reasonable idea of what they want to do after school, so they can see the benefits of schooling in that it will allow them to get where they need to be. They are able to tackle more challenging texts, concepts and ideas, so you get to read more adult texts with them. And of course they are more personable, funny, engaging and adult. Not all, of course, but most. You can still get the occasional bit of silly behaviour but you can get that in any area of society. School students do not have a monopoly on stupidity. If you get a Year ten class, you should aim to enjoy it and use the opportunity to teach. I know we teach in Years 7, 8 and 9, but you get the feeling that it really sticks for most kids in Year ten.

However, I must admit that I have had kids say that they were not going to really push themselves until they got to Year 11 as that's when it gets serious. Usually it is capable students who have this attitude and frankly some of them can actually bide their time and then put in a big effort in Year 11 and do quite well in the VCE. Some students are naturally gifted and do not have to work on it. The trouble is, the other less capable students catch onto this idea and mimic it, often with disastrous results.

"But,' I hear you cry, 'shouldn't you be forcing these students to complete all work to the best of their ability all of the time?' Well maybe, but you try and force a student to do anything and see how you go. You can cajole, and encourage and argue logically that they would be better served by doing the work, but unless the student WANTS to do well, they won't. So the big trick is getting them to want to do well. 'How do you do this?' I hear you ask in plaintive tomes. (You are chatty today aren't you). Well it is hard. Look, this problem isn't just restricted to Year 10. I have known students in Year 12 who take this attitude to their studies. They think that if they really put in the work just before the exams at the end of the year, they will do well. You just need to plug away with some students. They get the message eventually.

One of the best things that happened to me was when I had a year ten student quit school at the start of the year. He was one of those kids who always disliked school and didn't really do much work. He was a bad influence on other students even though he was a nice kid. It was just that others caught his lethargy. He left school to become an apprentice roof tiler. It was near the start of the year as I said, and it was a particularly hot year. After two weeks he was back. He actively went around to all of the other students and told them to stay in school as it was 'Hell out there'.

So you could send them all out tiling roofs in summer to make them do some work.

<u>Year 11</u>

Good texts, focused students, mature minds and pretty well embedded skills. What could go wrong? This is teaching so, you know, don't get complacent. Year 11 is another transitional year. Yes they are completing Units and 1 and 2 of VCE, but do they really matter? Isn't it just the results of your SACS and exam in Year 12 that count towards your score? Haven't we been doing the same basic topics since almost Year 7? Do we really need to worry too much about Year 11 results?

These are just some of the points you will have to reckon with in Year 11. Maturity wise, this is not unlike Year 10. A little bit older and a little bit wiser. But also, a little bit more likely to be working a part time job and a little bit more likely to be partying till all hours. Again, teaching Year 11 is a good gig. Lots more maturity, hardly any poor behaviour apart from laziness and you don't have the responsibility that comes with a Year 12 class. I mean you have all of the usual responsibilities and you have an obligation to make sure the students are Year 12 ready, but the opening statements are correct. The Year 11 exams do not matter beyond getting them ready for Year 12.

By now a lot of the students who hate school will have dropped out, gone to TAFE or they will be working somewhere. Some teachers go to visit the ones who have a job just for the unique pleasure of actually seeing them work. So you will have a class of keen students raring to get to grips with those tricky texts and concepts. Or not.

Our school, like many others has an accelerated program where gifted students are placed in a class in Year 7 and that class is given work that is considered at least a year above the mainstream classes. They are accelerated in other words. It is a good system. These students are often highly competitive and they push each other to improve. Some of them are very bright indeed. However, those accelerated classes merge with the mainstream classes in Year 11. I have taught Accelerated Year 10 classes and I have then taught a Year 11 class with many of those same accelerated Year 10 students in it. They know most of the mainstream kids of course and you get the feeling that they look around the other students in their Year 11 class and they think, 'These guys are useless. I can cruise in this class.' Remember I said they were competitive? Well this is where it falls away. I guess it is like an Olympic runner being pitted against a high school champion. The Olympic runners just think, 'Well it is going to be easy to beat these guys', and they just cruise. So again, your main job is to cajole and encourage and point out that 'These skills will have a direct result on your year 12 results.' All you can do is push.

Year 11 is like the butterfly, drying out its wings and getting ready to fly. Which makes Year 7 and 8 the grub stage, and Years 9 and 10 the closed up cocoon. Probably needs a bit of work as far as analogies go, but you get the drift. Our newly formed butterfly is a social animal. Or insect.

There are parties, trips away with slightly older friends who have a car and of course there is the senior formal.

The Senior Formal is a social event for the Year 11 and 12 students. It is a chance to dress up in all of their fineries (That butterfly analogy is doing really well here) and flaunt themselves on the world stage. Well, the dance floor of the local hall or whatever. The girls will all look spectacular, which is only to be expected as they seem to spend the previous three weeks getting ready for the night, and the boys all look sophisticated and mature. It is usually a really great night. Staff get to wander around confiscating alcohol and smiling benignly, as the students inexplicably get drunk. Then at the end of the night new romantic attachments have formed, and all the staff have to do is wait for parents to come and pick up the last of the revellers.

The work that the students have to complete is challenging and should be setting them up to do well in Year 12. This is where the fatigue with the curriculum kicks in. I really think we need to reassess the way we teach our students. The results that we were getting even ten years ago were better than the results we are getting today. I am no fan of data, but the data points to the fact that results are trending downwards. Yet we persist in this idea that teaching students the same skills each year will lead to improved results and this idea just does not stack up. The students are bored, the teachers are bored and exhausted and the results are just not there. I think this needs a rethink by the Education Department, but what would I know.

When I was in Year 11, I can remember we studied 'Macbeth'. It turned me onto Shakespeare and I have been a fan all of my life (Thanks Mr Hardie). These days we still study 'Macbeth' in Year 11 and it is one text that I feel deserves to have been kept on. (We only just got rid of 'Lord of the Flies'!) We even still watch Roman Polanski's film version. It brings back memories for me. The students seem to pick up on my passion for the text and they end up enjoying it.

I think this says a lot about the power of passion in teaching. If you cannot feel passionate about a text, or a unit of work, I think you owe it to students to at least fake the passion. I know that sounds dishonest, but I have seen the excitement levels of a class get killed by a teacher expressing disdain for a text they are about to study. Be passionate. If you are not passionate, pretend to be. You need to sell the text sometimes.

Again I can't talk for other subjects but Year 11 English has some good texts. They have more complex ideas and often deal with quite adult concepts and the kids appreciate this. They feel we are treating them like adults by studying these texts.

I also owe one very significant teaching moment to my very first Year 11 class. They were a nice bunch of kids mostly and quite bright. There was one boy who was the class clown and he just mucked around a bit too much (Hi Pat). I constantly had to have one to one chats with him outside the class so that I didn't disturb the others. When you have these one to one chats outside of the classroom, always face the interior of the classroom so you can see what is going on. We were chatting away and I noticed that the whole class just disengaged from what they had been working well on and started chatting. I finished talking to the student and walked back in and realised that whenever I talked to Pat, it meant I was neglecting the other students. It wasn't a big deal, but I did cut down my one to one sessions from then on.

One other point to watch out for is the fact that you will get a bit of attrition in Year 11. The students reach the point where they are legally allowed to leave and you find a few just seem to disappear. Most hang around for the first term, but when the SACs begin to appear and there is some real work to be done, a few drift away. It is far easier for them to get employment during the year, than at the end when all of the other students are leaving school and looking for jobs.

Toward the end of the year, the Year 11 students begin the subtle change into year 12 students. They have to pick the design for their Year 12 top, (but that might just be our school) and there will be interviews for School captain applicants for the following year. The Year 11s start to eye off the Year 12 study/common room and its microwave and toasters. Yes, things are beginning to get serious.

Head start classes. For a couple of weeks at the end of the year, the Year 12 teachers for the following year sit down for hours and hours and plan meticulous 'HeadStart' classes for the Year 11 students to ignore. Most will turn up for the first class, where astute teachers hand out everything they think will be important. Many will turn up for the second, and then after that it is a bit of a raffle. The serious kids will turn up. The rest won't as they switched off about the time of the senior formal.

I think that's about it for Year 11. Important, but not quite as important as Year 12. It's not really a ringing endorsement is it?

Year 12

School Assessed Coursework and exams. And that's it for Year 12!

No just kidding. The start of the new school year is very exciting for the Year 12 cohort. They have their own study centre where they can heat lunch, have coffee, play games, chat and read if they feel like it. Oh and Study! Yessiree Bob there will be a whole lot of Studying going on. Funnily enough some students do study. I would not have bothered to point that out ten years ago, but things have really changed for our Year 12 students since then.

What you are about to read is called Year 12 whingeing. You will hear it whenever two or more year 12 teachers gather together in the photocopy room.

"They don't work as hard as they should."

"They have not even read the book."

"Ten years ago we used to have good discussions in class. These kids know nothing!"

"Homework? They don't do that."

Etc. etc.

It is a bit sad and it is true. There has been a fundamental change in the way that students approach their last year of Secondary school. Way back when (i.e. ten years ago) many of the students actually read the English texts being studied. Some of them had even read them twice! And one or two may have even made notes! It is different now. I am assuming it is the same for other subjects, but it is most disheartening to front up to the first class of the year and the students have not completed the holiday homework handed out during the head start classes, and it becomes painfully obvious that only one or two, IF YOU ARE LUCKY, have read the texts.

There are reasons for this. The diminished status of the ATAR (Australian Tertiary Admission Rank) score at the end of the year. Lots of universities do not put a lot of store into the ATAR believing that it does not accurately reflect a student's true abilities. It is basically a combination of the student's results in SACs and in the Exam at the end of the year. Because of this, many students don't put a lot of faith in the ATAR either and, given that many are choosing not to go to University, they do not need it anyway, so they go 'unscored'. This means once they have successfully completed all of the school assessed work, they have passed. They do not have to sit the exam. The number of students who decide to go unscored has risen at our school each year and I assume that it is the case with most other schools in Victoria. So you end up with a block of students in each Year 12 class who are not taking it all seriously and who either chat away or just don't bother turning up.

I once had one student who decided to go unscored at the start of the year, then changed their mind about three weeks out from the exam. He asked me what he should do. I advised the invention of a time machine, go back, do the work, and then do the exam. He seemed unimpressed. This actually happens a lot. Students suddenly realise that the big wide world is a real place that values official bits of paper saying you have certain skills and they decide they want that piece of paper and try to cram a year's work into a few weeks.

I used to tell my Year 11 classes to surreptitiously watch the Year 12 students going into their English exam. I pointed out that the ones who looked just a bit nervous, had done all of the work and had completed practice exams and practice essays. The ones throwing up from anxiety, not so much.

The Year 12 program does get cut into a little bit during the year. They have the senior formal to attend and that is a social highlight of the year. They also have swimming sports and athletic sports and funnily enough, they attend these wholeheartedly as they realise it will be their last school sports day! They fact that most of them haven't attended in the last three years is by the by. They dress up and cheer and race with the best of them. They actually do not interact very much with the rest of the school population. If you don't teach Year 12 you don't exist really except as a sort of background character who once had them for Humanities in Year 8.

In fact it is odd how quickly each year level dismisses you once you have finished teaching them. Oh they will be polite and they will say hi, but you are not important to their world so you get short shrift. Of course then, when you don't expect them to even notice you, they are suddenly clamouring around you asking you if they were your favourite student back in Year 8. The correct response to this is 'Of course you were...Marty isn't it?'

They will enjoy their common room and they will enjoy the ability to wander down the street at lunchtime. (Actually they enjoyed that ability in Years 9, 10 and 11, but now they can do it legally.) They won't enjoy SACs and they definitely won't enjoy the practice exams in the term three holidays. The fact that their teachers enjoy it even less is small recompense.

However, there is one day that is more important than exam day. There is one event that puts the senior formal in the shade. It is the one day that binds all schools together. Muck up day....I'm sorry... We have renamed it. Celebration Day. That had to be a departmental idea. Muck up day at our school is tightly controlled. We had one muck up day that went a bit far with KFC gravy sprayed all over windows and doors (One of the kids worked there) and generally a real mess was made. This meant tight controls were placed on what the students could and could not do.

These days the students have to arrive at the school early for breakfast. Anyone who is seriously drunk is sent home. They are restricted to one part of the school. They can decorate rooms and corridors but only with easily cleaned up products. Then they perform a parade in front of a whole school assembly. Then they clean up and they are sent home.

However, before they get to the glories of muck up day and the fun of exams, they have their day to day classes. At this stage the students are not learning anything new. They are applying the skills they have learnt all the way through their schooling. Hang on... I had better rephrase that; At this stage the students SHOULD NOT be learning anything new. Let's face it, they have either forgotten half the things they have learnt along the way or they never really learnt those things properly anyway. So there is a bit of new learning going on for some of them.

I have had students in Year 12 swear black and blue that they have never heard of a particular concept. 'No Way. Did not happen!' And yet, I KNOW they have been exposed to this particular concept before because I taught them in Year 11 and/or in Year 10 when I know we not only covered that concept, I can even show them their SAC results on the piece of work that utilised that concept. This actually happens quite a lot in all year levels. And it isn't just from year to year.

Marty (Year 10) – I've never heard of this before.

Me – Marty we did it last term.

Marty – Well its news to me.

Me –

Class - Yeah we did it last term.

Marty – Well I don't remember it.

Me – Actually Marty we did it right at the end of last term as I knew we would be doing more of that work at the start of this term. So it was, you know, three weeks ago.

NOTE – I think Marty was having a pretty wild time during the end of term holidays.

Year 12 is a pretty full on Year because it really only goes for three full terms and then it is revision for three weeks in Term 4. It just flies by. The students are also busy with getting their licence to drive, getting a car, driving the car, working in two jobs to afford running the car, boyfriends and girlfriends who want to go for rides in the car and drinking. You know, all the usual teenager stuff.

At the end of the school year, the Year 12 students have a catered lunch at the school, and they invite any teachers who have taught them at any time in the secondary school life. This is always a pleasant occasion and students get the staff and each other to sign their shirts and dresses. I have no idea what they do with the items of clothing that has been signed. I mean, I presume they get washed. It is at this function that I distribute the 'Letters to their future self' that they wrote back in our old Humanities class in Year 7.

Sadly fewer and fewer of the students are there to get their letter as most have left before reaching the end of Year 12. However, those who do get to read their letter have later told me that it was a highlight of their last year at school. Some of them get teary and most get a real laugh out of what they wrote to themselves. I did try to get this made a natural part of Year 7, but I think it fell by the wayside when people realised just how few students continue on to complete Year 12. It is just as well that I made them write their home addresses on the envelopes as I can just send off the letters to those who are no longer at school.

Like Year 11, the final year of study has a mainstream and a VCAL (or VCE Vocational Major) stream. The two cohabitate the study room. The VCAL kids are often off campus at various TAFE course and work placements but they do spend a lot of time at the school and are just considered a part of the Year 12 cohort.

The last lunch together is pretty much the last time they will be together. Most of them are there for the English exam, but not all of them. So the last lunch can get a bit emotional for some students. They do have one more formal occasion and that is the Valedictory Dinner. This is a great chance for teachers and parents to celebrate the end of schooling for the kids...oops, young adults.

And that's it for the year levels.

Uniforms

This is a contentious topic for many people. Some people think it is odd that we encourage students to be individuals and to chart their own course, but then we make them dress in a uniform. Others argue that it isn't the clothes that are important, it is the people that count. I have known teachers who believe in a strict adherence to the school's uniform policy and who chase up kids out of uniform at form assembly. This works if you have a coordinator who feels the same way and backs up the teacher.

On the other hand I have also known teachers and coordinators who are not so strict on the whole uniform thing. This can work too as long as the student makes some sort of effort to at least try and fit in with the uniform policy. Ok they are wearing sneakers, but they had the sense to blacken the white bits to fit in with the black shoes aspect of the policy.

The major problem occurs when you have a teacher strict on uniforms with a coordinator above them who is not overly fussed about the uniform policy. It is then up to the two of them to come to a working arrangement.

The enforced wearing of a uniform, means that some students whose parents cannot afford to buy expensive casual clothing are not discriminated against. The wearing of a uniform decreases the likelihood of 'fashion' bullying particularly by female students. I'm sorry of that sounds sexist, but it is the way it works.

When our school has casual clothes days, we always have a small group of students in each year level, who come in uniform. Either their parents make them, or they just don't have clothes that would be acceptable to the fashionistas. At least when in uniform they can just say that they forgot it was a casual clothes day and they will get left alone.

As I said, this is a contentious issue. You are best advised to follow the school rules. The school rules are a wonderful 'get out' for teachers. If challenged on anything that relates to school policy you just have to point to the school rules and say, 'If you have a problem you need to talk to the principal. I don't make the rules.' Which is a cop out of course but hey, they earn the big bickies for a reason.

Interviews

The following interviews are with people who have had a varied amount of time in the educational system. One is a highly respected, experienced teacher with many years of years of teaching at all levels. One is a relatively new teacher who is in his fourth year as a teacher and the third is an experienced teacher and Principal. I chose these three people because I value their opinions and they have impressed me with their thoughts and how they work. I should point out that their inclusion in this book does not mean that they endorse or agree with the sentiments expressed by myself.

Cynthia

My first interview is with an experienced teacher. She has taught at a few schools and has earned a reputation as a skilled, passionate and caring teacher. She has held just about every position there is to hold in a school. She cares deeply about her students, her fellow staff and her profession.

<u>Why are you a teacher? What attracted you to the job? Why have you kept teaching?</u>

I've always loved children so it seemed logical to have a career that would revolve around them. I wanted to be a part of their formative years. I was attracted to the job because it was both valued by society and was progressive in nature. By teaching a child, I was contributing to (hopefully) a better future. I thought teaching would give me a lot of personal satisfaction where I could give something back to society. I was grateful for my lot in life, and I felt that I should be able to give back to others. I wanted children to understand that education is their way forward. It is not about consumerism, or materialism, it is about learning so that they have choices and understanding. By learning about others, children can learn about themselves. As clichéd as it sounds, I wanted to develop life-long learners.

<u>So you're not doing it for the money?</u>

God, no! No way!

<u>What is the best part of the job? What is it that you love?</u>

The best part of the job, for me, is that light-bulb moment; when there is understanding. I think that is the most joyous part. It's that moment when you teach something to children and they 'get it'. They understand and you see the fruits of your labour. So much effort goes into the planning behind the teaching of a concept or a skill and then, when you see the final result and you think, 'Yes! You've understood the message I've tried to get across to you. It's worked!' Another thing I really enjoy is to see those children who have struggled and, years later, they come back to you and say, "I never really appreciated what you did for me then, but I do now." Some even apologize. Those are really joyous moments because you have had an impact on someone's life. You can't put a monetary price on it because there isn't one.

<u>What are the worst aspects of the job?</u>

How many reasons can I give? Let's see now: the correction. People don't understand the time it takes to read, edit, provide feedback then follow up with reporting, parent-contact, Compass -and that's only for those who have actually submitted the work. Furthermore, correction is an imposition on your family who often take second place because of the job. My husband repeatedly says that unless you live with a teacher, you have no idea what is involved. Your mind is always on the job. When you go to bed at night you are thinking about lesson plans or that parent who has a concern about a child or the work you have to do the next day. You never really switch off. Even during school holidays, you are reading the novels, you're still preparing for the next year. It is always ongoing.

The other element of teaching that has changed for the worse is the pressures of time. The amount of testing done at the expense of teaching has led to data being the golden measure to assess a child's needs. What rot. I remember a VATE lecturer warning us to never let a child be reduced to a number in a box.

Furthermore, we don't see staff volunteering as much today. There used to be a 'swings and roundabouts' approach to running schools but now it's a case of "I'll do this for you, so long as there is something in it for me.' You have to compensate people for working on camps or walking around the town putting leaflets into letterboxes to promote an Art Show. Well, I don't teach Art, but my family regularly helped to drop leaflets, let alone volunteer for Front of House on Exhibition Night so that I might support the Art Faculty and the school. It's harder to get that volunteer support and I understand why, because it keeps taking time away from your own interests and family. But schools have lost that community feel which has a ripple effect on staff/student relationships.

How has teaching changed?

The introduction of technology has certainly created a different teaching environment. I wouldn't say it has revolutionised teaching, because technology has its advantages and disadvantages. It allows quicker sharing of resources but also provides 24 hour access to Staff. Teachers are doing more administration and less thinking about how to make the concept they are teaching to the class, enjoyable. Today, they are expected to uploaded daily lesson plans, know every child's ILP and make immediate contact with parents when there are issues.

In the past, we were trusted to prepare lessons tailored for our students. Not anymore. I also think the reporting that you are giving back to the parents is more generic. It is less personal and individualised.

The feedback is jargonised. People make banks of quotes and just plug them into the reports, and we are doing the kids and parents a disservice in that. It is meaningless feedback really. Furthermore, the impact of social media has certainly impacted upon classroom behaviours. To be fair, the ban on mobile phones helped this situation; although students have already worked out ways to get around the restrictions.

I resent the time it takes to deal with administration issues. Anything that happens has to be recorded so it can be used as evidence in some way. You have to record everything, which takes a lot of time. Naturally, you're robbing Peter to pay Paul, so this time affects the amount of creativity you inject into the preparation of class lessons.

Another change is the impact of helicopter parents. These are parents who contact you and want to quiz you to the nth degree as if they know more about your subject than you. They don't trust you. And very often, they haven't really read what you have had to say about their child's learning. They look at assessment percentages and make criticisms about a teacher's competency. By extension, I believe teachers are unfairly blamed for many social issues and have lost a lot of public respect.

<u>How could you make the job better? If it was up to you and you had the power, what would you do?</u>

I don't know. You are asking a simple question, but it requires the community of the school. We are very fragmented at our school, and I suspect that all institutions are the same situation where spacial issues have literally divided the staff, so their desks are not in the same space anymore. This means we don't incidentally socialise anymore. Currently, our social staff room is only used by CRTs-it's like a ghost town and is a far cry from the hub-bub of the 90's.

As a result, you don't get that bonding with other staff and by extension, that sense of community amongst the staff. As said previously, so you don't get that volunteering to help and support each other, and that flows into the classroom. Significantly, you don't feel that you are valued. Instead, you are a worker who contributes to the running of the school, but we have lost that bigger picture of valuing all staff and creating a sense of community. So, in my dream school, I would devote one or two larger space to a work room and another as a separate social space.

Secondly, I would give staff more time to work on the core job of classroom preparation and marking. Over the years, our Staff Meetings are less about students and more about policy. I can assure you that many eyes glaze over at the PowerPoints.

How will teaching change in the future? Not necessarily where you would like it to go, but where it will go?

I have a strong gut feeling that we will become a virtual school. Society will always need 'babysitters' and children are always going to need a place to physically learn to mix with others. But, if we become a virtual school, how will we monitor the growth of students? We will have to teach them to work independently. Children don't do that naturally. It is a skill. I suspect that in the future, students will be able to sign up to classes that they are interested in, at places they want to go to, and they might not even be attending the same school all of the time. They might do English at one school and Maths at another, and Drama at yet another school. It will be like university where you pick your subjects, and you will pick the timetable that suits you and at what time of the day it suits as well. I don't think schools will run from 9 am until 3.30 or 4pm. I think they will operate from 9am till 9 pm. This will open education up to suit mature aged students as well. Already, our school is losing a senior student who is going to study at the Virtual School of Learning.

Do I think this will be an improvement? No. I think kids need to be in front of a teacher. When students returned to class from remote learning (COVID), I realised just how much of a difference there is between a real classroom and the virtual one. The virtual classroom is a lonely place.

What about the impact of Artificial Intelligence (AI) in the classroom?

I'm not sure about AI. I think it undermines our kids' confidence where they are losing security in their own abilities. Students feel better if they can use AI to help them with their homework. This has two ramifications: They don't trust their own intelligence. It used to be that creativity occurred in the classroom. You would do it with students and they would build confidence in their skills, but now they don't trust themselves to do the work. AI is so cold and impersonal so staff can tell when work is AI generated. And this leads to the second issue of authenticity, so sadly, we waste more time validating the originality of student work.

Have students changed?

I don't think children have changed per se, but their needs have become quite diverse. They appear to be more literal than they have ever been before, and I'd say social media has significantly contributed to this. Their waning interest in reading and wanting to know about the issues in the world has contributed to secondary problems and wider social ignorance. Autism, anxiety and ADHD are common medical traits, but rising poverty with its associated marital breakups and emotional repercussions seems to impact upon our role as teachers.

On the flip side, however, some students are quite entitled, and they have been allowed to get away with it where Staff (and parents) seem quite at a loss at knowing how to respond because children don't understand the consequences of their actions. The way the 'f-bomb' is regularly a part of their vernacular and is a measure of their ignorance. Kids are still kids. They will always try you, but it is the way we respond to their behaviour that has changed. I don't think we are as consistent in our approach, and kids appear more confused and entitled.

How has teaching changed you?

I don't think it has fundamentally changed me. I think I am more appreciative of those who contribute to the development of others. I am aware of how much it has taken from my family, of that, there is no doubt. My kids are not joking when they say they will never be teachers: they have told me that bluntly. It is a job that takes and takes and takes. It gives back, but not commensurate to what you put into it.

Teaching has made me more aware of my strengths and my weaknesses. I remember my supervisor during my first teaching round warning me that this job has the capacity to leech as much out of a person, as does building them up. "Be careful that you don't care too much, because they're the teachers who don't survive.' I said, 'What do you mean by that?' And he told me that I would know once I started teaching. And I do understand that now because teaching can become all consuming.

The best part of teaching is meeting the people I have met along the way, both children and adults. Most of my closest friends are teachers because we share the same values, and we care about the same things. I love the fact that teaching allows a person to keep on learning about everything: technology, other subjects. I enjoy it.

I must confess that after teaching Year 12 English for almost 35 years, I am totally disillusioned with post-secondary education. Philosophically, I cannot tell Year 12 students to pursue a tertiary education and chain them to a life of debt. Courses are more expensive, they last longer (teaching is now a six-year tertiary qualification), and the fixed interest on HECs sees students start their mid-twenties well behind their trade apprentice peers where their debt increases as they begin working, as a result of high inflation. This madness at making education a choice only for the wealthy seems very divisive and I can no longer subscribe to it.

<u>What makes a good teacher?</u>

Someone who is consistent, fair, and has the child's best interests at heart.

<u>What advice would you give to a new teacher, or to someone considering teaching as a profession?</u>

To be honest, I wouldn't recommend teaching as a career. I used to think of it as a Calling, but the costs seem too great.

Advice: If you say something, you must do it. Don't say something if you are not going to keep that promise.

Establish a routine, from the very beginning. And make that routine fair to both you, and the environment in which you are working.

Know the parameters. I have never succeeded in this area, and I wish that I was able to 'switch off' a bit more. Marking an English response may mean that you have so many criteria to consider that it could take you 30 minutes to correct one essay. If you have 120 students, it is not sustainable. Ironically, almost every English teacher I know is a part-timer. So, if you are going to be a teacher, be aware that it is a profession that will eat into your private life. My advice is to have to have another outlet other than teaching. If you don't, it becomes all-consuming and that's not healthy.

<u>Can a person be taught to be a good teacher, or does it require a certain personality?</u>

I think you do have to have a certain personality. I don't think it is something you can teach, it is inherent. A good teacher...You can see it. Furthermore, you will know if you want to be a teacher. If you are just doing it because it is a job, you will not survive. It is healthy to have doubts, to question yourself. But I just think there are some people who think teaching is easy and all they do is go to school and look after kids for an hour. We know it is not that. It is all the work that goes beforehand and all the work that comes after. What you do in the classroom ...That's the entertaining 'acting' part. It's The Performance. Everything else is hard yakka. You need to know how to deal with the controversy and the conflict that comes with the job. There are some damned good teachers, who have left the profession well before retirement age because of the demands required of today's teacher.

Nathan

In his fourth year of teaching, Nathan has had his first taste of teaching Year 12 classes this year. He is a friendly person who has found it easy to build a rapport with students.

<u>Why are you a teacher? What attracted you to teaching? Why have you kept teaching?</u>

I think, in the most pragmatic sense, I don't know what else to do with my life, as sad as that might sound. I have tried a few different things in my life and somehow I always kept coming back to teaching as being the thing that might bring me some fulfilment. I have always been a fairly curious person. I like to learn, and so I thought there might be a chance I could impart that to students.

(Here, we were interrupted by a student wanting to talk to Nathan, which seemed entirely appropriate)

I was attracted to the job because I really like structure and routine. I like that it is laid out for me in that I know what I will be doing next year. I know what that looks like in terms of time, and I know what my days will look like. Before this I was working in construction where I could get a phone call at 8 o'clock at night saying I was working in Springvale tomorrow or wherever. I like that the stability of the job continues through the year. It is not a case of three months' work and then some time off and you don't really know how long that will last. It's a yearlong process. You know you are working. You know you are getting paid and you know you are getting paid the same amount every week for a year. When I started the economy was not as bad as it is now, but there was this sense that having a stable pay check was going to make life easier.

I have kept teaching because I have come to enjoy this job more and more. There are things that have kept me in this job and there is also that sense of not knowing what else I might want to do with my life. In a perfect world I wouldn't want to work at all. I'd like to stay home and carve wood and read and write and do my hobbies. So there is this sense of if not this, then what? So it's this.

<u>What are the best parts of Teaching? What is it that you love?</u>

School Holidays. That is really nice. I mean, I'm going to Japan in January and we are planning overseas holidays for next year. We are going during the end of term break so that means we keep getting paid and that doesn't happen in other jobs.

But, if I look at things on a day to day basis, the thing that really surprised me the most was the relationships you build with the students. I just finished a Year 12 class that had many students from my first Year 9 class a few years ago.

In that last class, I was getting really sentimental which is not something that I expected. I didn't know I had that response in me. There have been a lot of students that I have grown to really like. You get to know them, and you get to know things about them. You get to see them grow up. I didn't think that was something that would resonate with me as much as it has. That has been a really fulfilling part of the job.

The staff are also a part of the attraction. Everyone is educated. I think you have to be a relatively interesting person to actually get into this job. The people that you meet are awesome. I mean I met my girlfriend here so...there is that. I've made some really good friends.

I like that it is different. Every day is just different. Imagine being a doctor and sitting in that one room and every fifteen minutes someone new walks in and they are sick and whingey. Here, every day is just different. And yeah, sometimes they are not great days, but they are different and I need that. I need something different to keep working towards. If I were a mechanic, I'd be coming in every day, fixing a car and then leaving...Does nothing for me. In other jobs I have had, you watch the clock. You sit there and you think "I've got four hours to go" You don't do that here.

<u>What are the worst parts of the job?</u>

I do not like the fact that this job does not fit into a seven or eight hour day is the obvious one I think. You can't do everything that needs to be done to actually help kids improve. For a lot of this I have a bit of a fatalistic view. A lot of kids are just going to get better because that's what they do, and a lot aren't, whether they had me, you or my Dad teaching them. It might not matter.

I like to think that what I am doing...The effort I put in, my style and all of those sorts of things mean that I do help kids improve. But at the same time, I see a kid for a couple of hours a week. What can I realistically do?

I am aware that as a teacher you might say just one thing that could have a significant impact on a kid's life. And that's great. Lately I have been more aware of trying to be a positive presence in people's lives because, who knows what they've got going on behind the scenes. If I can just be a nice part of their day that they don't dread coming into, well that's positive as well. The time is the obvious one. Not having the time to do all of the things we want to do.

That is the one that has been manifesting with me mostly lately. The meetings. The total ineffectual nature of the meetings and the lack of focus that schools have. I mean we looked at the AIP (Annual Implementation Plan - see entry) on Tuesday and it is just a dreadful document. We can't just narrow down ... here's one thing we want to do at this school, let's do that well. And once we have got that one thing done well, we will keep implementing that and then focus on something else. In my four years of teaching I have so many initiatives come and go and I can only imagine what experienced teachers have seen come and go. We have spent all year working on Learning Goals, and I wouldn't be surprised if they were gone in two years' time. Or they will be somehow different or there will be something else we have to do. And all of that time has been taken away from just being able to work; how can I teach my kids a bit better or what can this group of teachers do to make this unit of work better. They can tell us that it has a PLC (Professional Learning Communities) but that disappears. I mean... Week 4 PLC meeting, and the next isn't until week 8 and we have a PLC focus? We don't actually think about it until we actually go to that meeting. In my own PLC group, out of the five teachers who are meant to be there, due to the nature of our group there are two; myself and another staff member. It just doesn't work a lot of this stuff.

I think the bit that's gets you is that if we simplified this job, the better it would be. If we narrowed our focus to a few things we could do something really special. Instead, we are being pulled in fifty different directions, and our focus just becomes so muddled that we don't achieve a quarter of what we could or would like to achieve.

And there are some feral kids. That's a part of the gig, but there are far fewer of those than there are good kids.

It wasn't that long ago you were a student. Do you think teaching has changed in that time? You obviously had a different perspective of teaching from the other side of the desk but is the job what you thought it would be?

A colleague once mentioned that she thought the students were becoming more like clients. I think I can get a sense of that. It feels like the dynamic between teacher and student has changed. Instead of being the person in charge, and the person we should trust and the person who should be able evaluate children and communicate with parents to say "Well here is what is happening and here is what you need to do about it', we now have a jumble of perspectives and we are now 'working collaboratively with the parent' and all that. I feel like the power of the teacher is being diminished. I don't mean that you want to stand up there and be a tyrant and punish. I just feel the importance and the standing of the teacher is diminished. You are just seen as someone who looks after the kids for a couple of hours a day. But you also get "Well what are you doing? How come my kid isn't learning?' as opposed to 'Well, what is the kid doing?' Can we put the focus back on them because we are doing our job. Most of us are doing what we need to do and all of these extra demands mean that we don't get to do that job as well as we'd like to...Or, we just not trusted, to do that properly, because a parent doesn't like what we are doing or we are not following a certain program.

I was always amused in parent interviews when they wanted to know why their child was not progressing. I mean, I would only see them three hours a week in group of 24 kids. What are you doing at home?

I also get parent teacher interviews where there is this disconnect between how I see a student, and how the parent sees them. I wasn't bad at school but I was a little disinterested and my parents knew I was. They were under no illusions that I wasn't putting in my best effort. They knew I was chatty and distracted and that school was not my focus. That was not a shock to them or my teachers, so everyone could work together and so, if I could get this task done, we were all happy. But I get these parents come in and the portrait they paint of their children is just not what I see in the classroom, for better or worse. I've got parents telling me how bad their children are, and I say, well they sit there and they do their work and they try. And they say 'Well I've got them going to a speech therapist and this that and the other...' and I say, 'Your kids are standard. I've got a lot worse in my class. Your kids are fine and you're telling me all the things they can't do.' And you have the other extreme where you have complete rascals and butter wouldn't melt in their mouth at home. Maybe it's a lack of trust. I don't know. I just don't think the teacher is seen as significant as perhaps they once were.

How could you make the job better?

There are two things and it will never be both and it is unlikely that it will be either one or the other. It has to be more money, or fewer hours' face to face teaching. And I don't mean this one hour less a week that they put out last year that has somehow meant I am in the classroom more. I am doing more this year than I was last year! You've got to give me two to three classes and that's it. That's all I teach and that's my focus.

Not a fourth class, and not a G4L (Growth for Learning) class or something that I am teaching with another teacher. I know there is a shortage and they have to fill spots but it is all too much. We are juggling this enormous amount. How can anyone do as good a job as they could? I think this is why you see, particularly with English teachers, so many have gone part time. I'm only four years into my career and I'm already thinking that five years down the track I will be part time at .8. Whether that's because I have had children or because that's what I have to do to stay in the job.

One thing that has kept me going is that this year I am teaching a VCAL (Victorian Certificate of Applied Learning) class and the expectations are lower. They don't want constant feedback, they just want a score and that makes my life a bit easier. That's what has kept my head above water this year. Other than that I am flat stick. I've got four English classes and a G4L. It is an enormous amount of work and I think, thankfully, I am someone who doesn't procrastinate. I get to work and I do what I have to do and it is rare that I do much at home. Now that my Year 12 class has finished I don't do anything at home. I really try not to but I can see why people do.

That's the main one for me. The money would be cool and that would keep us all going a bit but at the same time we make a decent amount of money. I am fine with the money. But can I keep doing what I am doing when I have children? When I am a bit older and maybe my priorities change... Could I do what I do now? I don't know.

To throw in something else, I always say that if this job didn't have meetings, I would stay full time forever. If I could leave at 3.30 every day I would stay full time forever. That won't happen. Meetings have to exist in some form. There are things we need to do, I understand that. If there was just less we had to do, generally...That would make it better.

How will teaching change in the future? Not what you would like to see happen but what will happen?

I think this AI (Artificial Intelligence) thing is not good. There are already mixed ideas about how it should be used. There are people who think it should be used for brainstorming. That's the last thing I want it used for because I want the students to think. Reading and writing, whatever, they can all write like Shakespeare in phonetic language, I don't care, if that is what it came to. I might not like it but civilisation would continue. But if we can't think...what are we here for? I worry about that. Who knows? That might not age well if in three years it has disappeared.

It is hard to speculate about the uses of technology in education. We still don't know how to use laptops and phones effectively.

I think phones are actually going to start being used. Take my VCAL class for example. I can set a research activity on the laptop, it won't get done. I can do that so that they use their phone and those kids will work harder than I've seen them work all year. I don't know what it is. We are all guilty of the same thing. If you need to Google something you don't break open the laptop, you use your phone and you will do it then and there. I think there are ways the phone can be used for good and I think there will be a bit of a backflip on phones, and they will come back and be used in some capacity.

I think we as teachers will continue to be diminished. I think we will become more of an educational facilitator. *(Here we were interrupted by another student who needed to see Nathan. I guess we should have seen that one coming.)* With G4L, when that was first introduced as a replacement for Multi-Purpose Periods, they wanted to call us 'Learning Coaches' and the future will be more like that. This idea that we will help you find your potential and discover what it is you like.

(Here yet another student needed to talk to Nathan about Year 12 English as she was going to be in his class the following year. We should have seen this coming...Again!) So anyway, Learning Coach or facilitator whatever they tell us we are, I think at the end of the day we have to

be someone who specializes in an area to really do well at this. And I wonder if that is going to diminish more and if we are going to end up more like a labourer on a jobsite. Do a bit of this and a bit of that and maybe look after a science class and Maths class and be a 'My screens locked, come and fix it' type of role.

Many people complain that students today are lazier, or more entitled. Given it wasn't so long ago that you were a student, do you think they have changed?

I have discussed this with a colleague who taught me and we have chatted about some of the people who were at school, as students, with me and I've said that they were what I would consider 'bad' kids. Young offenders essentially. I can look back and I think that a lot of today's kids couldn't hold a candle to all those kids. They were proper 'wrong 'uns'. However I think, from what I understand and what people have told me, it is just the apathy that is the problem. It is so prevalent.

The fact that they can't fail, we can't keep anyone back means that they know they don't have to do anything. They can sit on their arse and get zeros all year long and then move to the next class. We've got them to Year 11 at a minimum. We are hamstrung by the department in that regard. All of the things like inclusion and well-being that students can use as a get out of jail free card to get out of the work they are meant to do.

That's the main difference. We were chatty, I could get distracted and do this and that but there was not an assignment I did not hand in; there was not a worksheet I didn't complete, eventually. There was nothing that I didn't do, eventually. And that's what I'm seeing, that lack of accountability that the students are held to.

And I saw this wellbeing thing start to come in when I was in Year 11, or Year 12. They pulled me aside, and I don't know why but maybe because I was from a divorced home or whatever it was. They sat me in this lounge chair and said 'Hey man, if you want to come in here and chill out sometimes, that's cool.' And even as a student I thought 'This is not good. There are going to be some kids who are going to take this for a ride.' And I didn't want to do it. I didn't want to be in there. I just wanted to do my classes and go home. That's all I wanted.

I think all of these things mean that the kids have got all of these ways to not actually do what they need to do. And I think it is showing.

I hypothesize a lot about this...For one, social media has just culturally knackered the kids. Personal achievement is far outweighed by how people perceive them. They are more worried about how people perceive them than by what they are actually achieving, which is a problem.

There are a lot of parents now, who just don't think school is worthwhile. And maybe they have fallen into the same trap. 'All you've got to do is make money and do this and this...' And in an area like this, well, opportunity is waning. And education is one way that you can set yourself up in a really good way to do well or at least give yourself a few options. Or at least have a fighting chance.

<u>You have said that in five years' time you will still be teaching which makes my question about will you still be teaching redundant.</u>

If we go back to the question about the best parts of the job, the good outweighs the negative. There are a lot of negatives about the job but I've got some good role models around here who sort of let me know by saying, 'Hey. Don't make these things bigger than they are.' And I am aware that every job has got some stuff that is just dumb, and annoying and inconvenient but that is stuff I've tolerated for four years and I seem pretty happy to continue to tolerate. I've not had that line in the sand moment where I've asked if I am going to leave. Am I going to keep doing this? Can I keep doing this? And I don't know what it would be for me to make that happen. Most things in this job I am pretty open to. So, five years, I'll be here, slogging away.

<u>Has teaching changed you at all?</u>

I've had to mature. I've always been a step or two behind everyone else. I get there eventually. Do well, eventually, but I've always taken that little bit longer. And I noticed that when I got here. I was jokey, jokey and stuffing around and you don't get to do that in a lot of ways. You don't get the time and it's not appropriate. And when you do start to understand that these kids, whether they want to or not, see me as a role model and everything I do, not just the whiteboard stuff, is teaching. My presence is teaching and the way I act is teaching. If I don't want teenage boys to be feral, I have to show them a better way. If I can show young people that there are really a lot of benefits to reading, to being nice to people, to showing respect to people, because, if nothing else, it is going to make your life a lot easier. Not for all of the nice things that happen for you as well but because life's a lot easier when people like you, because they think you are a pleasant person. I think that's an important thing.

Teaching has made me consider the way I was acting and being perceived by people. It has made me mature. It has made me interact with people a lot better. I worked in retail for a long time so I have always been good at things like de-escalation because you have to...I've seen a lot of conflict in my life and the less the better as far as I am concerned. I've always been good at that sort of thing, but you see it in a lot of different ways in teaching. Whether it's a young girl who comes into your class on the edge of tears...That's something I could never have handled four years ago and its old hat now. And the boys who are at each other's throats and a fight might break out. Being able to stop those things because you can read people has changed me a little bit as well. Just because I'm exposed to it so much more every day.

Can you teach someone to be a good teacher? Or is it something innate to someone's personality?

I think without the personal touch, this can't work. In layman's terms, I think that someone who is less intelligent, but better with people is going to be better than someone who is incredibly knowledgeable, but can't get through to people. If someone is not sociable, often they can't learn to be. It might be something they missed growing up or it's not in them to begin with and how do you teach that? How do you teach basics like looking someone in the eye and saying hello? How do you say "If everyone is having a conversation, just nod your head and chuckle. Don't jump in and try to make a fool of yourself. Just be a pleasant person to be around and don't make people dread speaking to you." How do you teach that?

If someone can't do that, teaching is just going to be difficult. There are people who have an easier time than others because they are very personable and are a positive influence. The kids will come and chat to them and feel comfortable and they'll think "Oh because I've sat here for five minutes and I've had a chat, you know what? I'll attempt this work.

I'll do this assignment.' Or they will decide that they like this teacher, he or she seems nice, so I'll listen when they speak or I'll try because they haven't got my back up against them for some weird reason.

If you can't build a rapport with students you have got nothing to fall back on. The amount we can just coerce students to do because they just like us... I mean, I'm sitting here doing this interview because I like you. I am sitting here with a teacher that I liked and I respected and maybe that will be me for someone one day. I think without that stuff teaching just doesn't happen

Brett

Brett has been a Principal for many years in a variety of schools. He has only been at his current school for a year and a half.

<u>Why are you in education? What attracted you to teaching?</u>

I've always had a sport background. I am from a family of real estate agents, and they were quite shocked when I went to university to study Arts, and I studied arts more because I didn't really know what I wanted to do and I just wanted to leave a door open. I went from school to uni, not vocationally, but more just to study. About halfway through my degree I realised I was going to have to start thinking about a career and teaching made sense. I still had a real love for sports, and I had two jobs while I was at uni. I was a bricklayer, and I worked for Cricket Victoria.

I enjoyed working with young people and seeing the enjoyment they got from what they were doing. Now I'm not going to lie. I hit the end of my degree, and had a year to go. Teaching had the attraction of lifestyle.

There was that illusion of twelve weeks holiday a year. Of course once you are in teaching you know that's not the case, but it is still attractive. I was also desperate to live overseas, in the UK, and twenty years ago it was common for teachers to go to the UK as they were screaming out for teachers. I taught and lived in London for a few years.

What attracted me to teaching was the love of sport, the fact that I really enjoyed the aspect of helping young people, and there was that lifestyle aspect. Given I was in my early and mid-twenties. I hadn't really thought long term. I didn't think of it as being the job I would do for the next fifty odd years. My view changed when I was in the UK.

I view myself now more as an educator, as opposed to a teacher. I've been a principal longer than I've been a teacher. When I was in the UK, in my third year, I fell into some project work, which was implementing specialist programs in primary schools in a borough of seventeen schools. This was back in the days of floppy disks (SH - I feel old in having to point out that these were a form of data storage) with a Primary to Year 6 PE (Physical Education) curriculum. I contacted a friend who was an Art teacher who had a floppy disk with the Art curriculum. So my role was to engage in project work to implement these curricula.

When I came back to Australia and returned to the classroom, I became pretty stale, pretty quick. I actually left teaching for two years and went and sold real estate. Then I came back to teaching and fell into various roles in schools doing projects and work for the department so my path to becoming a principal has been a bit different. And I suppose that's why I view myself as an educator more than a teacher.

I've had to learn a lot along the way as I probably didn't have that grounding that a lot of principals have in day to day teaching. I'm continually learning and I hope I'm transparent about that because I think that part of being a principal is showing that you are vulnerable, and the fact that that you don't know it all, is a great strength in being a leader. People might pretend that they know it all but they don't. And if I can show that, and that I am transparent about that, then I think that is a powerful aspect in my ability to continue as a principal.

<u>Given that your parents were not teachers, your only experience of teaching would have been when you were at school. Was there anyone who really impressed you? Whose teaching stuck with you in later life?</u>

There were two people. One goes back a long way. I finished prep, and my parents thought I had some sort of learning difficulty. I couldn't read, hated school, and struggled socially. Then I had a gentleman, Mr. Kuhne was his name. He was a young fellow, loved footy, loved cricket. He got to know me and I went from not being able to read, my phonic awareness was really quite poor, to by the end of grade 1 being top of the class and in the top groups. And that was through relationships. I never forgot that. I actually invited him to my wedding, and he came along. After I finished school and started teaching we became really good friends and he is still a good friend today.

The other person was a coordinator I had through Year 7 to Year 11 and we butted heads the whole time. It wasn't until I left and I'd been teaching and started to take leadership roles that I saw why he was the way he was. I couldn't understand it at the time, but the lessons I learnt from him have always held me in good stead. It helped me to realise that as leaders in schools, we need to make hard calls and we need to, at times, put the acid on students and parents, and staff for that matter, if it is in the best interests of our kids.

I learnt that from him.

<u>What is the best part of being a Principal? What do you love?</u>

First of all, I do love it. This is the third school I have been principal. Equally, I love seeing both students and staff grow. I've employed a lot of graduates over the years, and now, with a teacher shortage, we are employing fourth year pre graduates with permission to teach. To see these people grow and have 'ah ha' moments, for me, is just as good as seeing a student go from Year 7 through to Year 12. To see a teacher just flick a switch and think 'Yes. I get that now'; To see them more comfortable in the class; To have teachers who sit here in my office in tears and you get through that and they come and thank you saying your advice was invaluable or that they are grateful for the support you showed. I love that aspect of the job. We are in this to improve student outcomes, and to do that, we need our teachers engaged. Which isn't always the case.

I also love being a principal because I feel that we can have an impact on a grand scale. One thing we have done this year is to implement a different approach with our year 7 and 8 around applied learning, with hands on learning. It is good to see the impact that has had, not only for those students directly enrolled in that course, but also for the teachers who have those classes who get a bit of respite from when those students are out. The positive climate that has been created when those students are engaged has had a huge impact. And that is just one small example.

I've been fortunate to have helped set up two schools, or one school and one extra campus. I set up 'Flow' in Morwell and to have seen that over 700 students have been through "Flow", well it makes you proud. That's impact on a grand scale.

The other thing I love about being a principal, and this is a bit of advice that I'd give graduates and teachers who have been doing it for over fifty years, principals who are starting out or have been doing it forever, I really love celebrating the wins. We had our year twelves finish the other week. I was just watching them and seeing the joy on their faces and their teacher's faces...I don't think there are too many jobs where you get that cycle of joy. If you don't celebrate that, you can become really stale, really quick. I love that aspect of the job.

It is not easy. Being a teacher, being a principal, being an educator...Working in schools, working in the front office; being the daily organiser. It's not easy. Dealing with teenagers isn't easy so we need to celebrate those wins and I really love that.

What are the worst parts of the job?

One of them has to be, for me, dealing with irrational and confrontational parents and staff. I have kids myself and I understand that you are passionate about your kids. Staff are passionate about the kids in their class and the areas in which they teach. When we make decisions, we are not making those decisions to be nasty. We don't make decisions because we don't like a young person. We are making them in the best interests of the whole school and ultimately for that young person. In the moment, in my job, we do have to deal with a lot of confrontation. Since there have been reforms around staff safety, I've been pretty firm around the fact that we do not have to put ourselves at the forefront of confrontation. We've taken the hero factor out of being a school leader. We didn't get into this job to have arguments and blues with parents but sometimes you just have to go there.

That has been raised as the major issue facing principals across the state.

It is, and I feel for principals who feel they need to be everything to everyone the whole time.

You can't be. You need to protect yourself. In order to do this job, as a career, if you are always putting yourself on the firing line, you won't be able to.

The more transparent you are as leaders, the more understanding there is around decisions. At times you need to explain things in multiple ways, to multiple people whether it is staff or parents. If you are honest, and you show you care, and show you are genuine, and you are transparent over how the decision has been made, they generally come on board. It doesn't always happen, and that's the hard part.

The worst part of this job is when you lose a student.

<u>Unfortunately your first day ...</u>

Yes my first day at this school we had to deal with the loss of a student. Dreadful. There would be no worse aspect to the job than that. In other schools I've been in we've lost students as well and it never gets any easier. What you need to do is just be absolutely, totally genuine and show compassion, care and love, for the whole community.

<u>You have been a principal for some time, has the role of the Principal changed in that time?</u>

It has, and I think it will continue to change. When I first became a principal, there was this thread that principals were the instructional leaders of the school. You needed to be at the forefront and be an expert in teaching and learning. That role still exists but Covid has changed the game significantly. FISO 2.0 (Framework for Improving Student Outcomes) has come in, and you've got learning and wellbeing at the same level and the understanding that to have quality learning you have to have wellbeing at the same level. When I started teaching twenty odd years ago to talk about wellbeing and to explicitly teach behaviours was a foreign concept. Now, to have an understanding that wellbeing needs to be at the same level as learning, well that's not changing.

Six years ago at another school, I pulled out our yearly Professional Learning calendar and nine out of ten of the professional learning activities were teaching and learning based. I pulled out the same calendar for this school three months ago, and eight or nine out of ten of the activities were wellbeing based. A huge turnaround.

So we have teachers coming in who are trained to teach, but the expectation is now that we have to support the health and wellbeing of the kids, which we do have to do, but a maths teacher of thirty years standing, who is an expert mathematician has not got the same level of understanding as our wellbeing coordinator. That's been a big shift.

Another big change is that the importance of workplace safety has increased significantly, especially post Covid, and the workplace manager, which is how we are termed, needs to be across Occupational Health and Safety laws, staff wellbeing, Department of Education and Training policies and that is a landscape that is becoming more and more overwhelming. There is more responsibility on us as managers to provide a safe workplace. In terms of mental and physical health, this is extremely difficult when you have got 750 teenagers on site. It is an inherently stressful workplace. So a part of that is making sure we have the right conditions in place. Things will happen. We know that. The department knows that. But you need the pre-conditions to do everything you can to avoid something happening and of course, after an event, to offer support. That is a huge amount of work; Necessary work. And that is something that has changed significantly in the last ten years.

<u>What would make the job better or easier?</u>

More community respect and understanding of the difficulties of working with 750 teenagers, and respect and a greater appreciation for the profession. I know we are not in Japan and we are not in Finland, I understand that, but teaching was once a respected profession and it is not now.

Or it is not respected in the same way. That would make the job easier across the board. The other aspect of this is that we have an incredible workforce shortage right now and we want all of our teachers to be the best they can be. However, we have graduates coming out now that, through no fault of their own, have not got the skills that we require, simply because we have to take them into the workforce earlier than we normally would. We have other teachers who are continually working under trying conditions, because of this staff shortage, and they are probably not operating at their optimum because of the workload. Yet, we are still expected to continually reach targets around student outcomes

It is a difficult thing to admit, but schools will be employing teachers now, that would not have been employed five years ago. Principals have conversations with other principals. I'd say "I'm thinking of employing this person. How are they?' and the other principal might say something in the negative, and I would move on. Now it is very much what do I need to be aware of with this person? What do I need to do to support them? I'm going to employ them, because we have to, but at least now I have an insight into what we need to do to help them develop.

In a perfect world, if there was not a teacher shortage, and you might have ten or twenty people apply for a job, what would you look for in a teacher that you were thinking of employing?

I always look for life experience outside of teaching. That does not mean I wouldn't employ someone who has gone from school, to Uni, to teaching. But I really want to see some life experience there. I don't want them in a school bubble all the time. They need personality. They are going to be dealing with teenagers, so they need a personality that is going to accommodate that.

They need absolute core knowledge of their subject area. They need to know what they are teaching. I also like to see teachers who have got some tools in their pedagogical toolkit; what is the art of teaching? Do they understand the art of it? It is all very well to say that for some people it comes naturally, but what is it you are doing? And lastly, they need to be genuine.

There is a lot of stuff there that are soft skills. They also need a level of humour. It could be internal humour, humour in the staff room, humour with the kids would be great but it is not necessary. And of course we always do reference checks.

So that was in a perfect world, but now, you might just have one person apply for a position. How do you prioritise those elements you just listed? What are you willing to overlook?

We try to identify the red flags so we can put things in place. If there are red flags, and there aren't always, if there are deficits, or issues that we have identified through their application, their interview or through reference checks, then we have to ask ourselves how comfortable are we as a school to be able to support them? How will they fit into our team? How do we think they are going to get along with kids? How can they manage a classroom? And we weigh all of that up. They might not have this bit, or they might not have that but we can really support there. We are going to know those areas. So in order to go into this employment that we probably wouldn't have gone into in the past, we have an understanding of what we need to do in order to support people. It is a totally different way of employing them.

We have been quite fortunate at this school, but I know of a number of schools where they have had over a dozen permanent CRTs (Casual Relief Teachers) all year. So that's a number of classes that have not had a permanent teacher all year. Someone might send their child to school and in the morning, they look at their timetable for the day and they might have five CRTs that day.

They haven't got one permanent teacher. That is incredibly difficult when you are trying to implement initiatives across the school. You are trying to keep order and you are trying to have some behaviour management program in your school. And of course you are trying to educate! It is difficult.

What are the most important personal attributes a teacher needs?

I would say empathy is the key one. Teachers all come from different backgrounds. But let's not forget the fact that all teachers are educated. They've all been to Uni for four years. Often they might come from a different class background from the students in their class.

Empathy and understanding around that fact is crucial the minute those kids walk in the door.

Resilience, because it is bloody hard. The resilience builds up over time, but you need the ability to be able to inflate the tyres when unfortunately the job has deflated them is important.

Time management skills are critical, not only in and around your job but in how you balance your life. This is critical. We see a lot of burn out, we see a lot of teachers leaving in that first five years and we see a lot of principals who don't last twelve, eighteen months. So time management and life balance are important.

You need to be genuine, but you also need to be able to act in front of the class. It is performance. And that means you can decompress when you walk out of that class. If you are doing that performance the whole time you will burn out so you need the ability to switch it off as well as to do it.

And as I mentioned earlier, you need humour. That's in the staff room, with your colleagues. It can be with the kids obviously. I think you need that to stay sane.

<u>Have the students changed in the time you have been involved in education?</u>

I would say that they have; however, a lot of these statements that students have changed are said at the same time that we, as educators, have gotten older. So we get older, and we look back and we've got twenty years' experience since when I was at school. So my perspective is different. My parents will look back on the sixties and to them, they were different times. But they are different as well because they are into their seventies.

So I think kids have changed. There is that well-being aspect I mentioned earlier. Mental health issues in teenagers have spiked significantly, and we can't shy away from that. I also think that for the next ten years we will have a generation come through that has been impacted by remote learning. So when we have a cohort of students who are 'difficult' we will able to trace them back to the covid years. And the issues we will face will either be academic, or developmental, which will affect behaviours but there will clearly be gaps. There will be gaps socially, developmentally and academically and we need to be aware of that.

Have the teachers changed in that time? If so, how?

I don't want to generalise, because with everyone, this isn't the case, but the work ethic of the older generation is significantly different to the younger generation. Again, I don't want to generalise but with some younger teachers there is a sense of entitlement that wasn't there. Whether that is generational or not understanding the job, I think it is created by the fact that we are in a buyers' market now for teachers. If a teacher is not happy right now they can leave and get another job. That wasn't the case even five or ten years ago. You could have sixty or seventy people applying for a job. So if someone gets their next year's allotment and it isn't what they want, they'll say 'Nah, stuff it. I'm going to go.' It hasn't happened here touch wood. So yeah, teachers have changed in that way.

It is not all doom and gloom. We have this tendency to say that the Universities do a terrible job and the teachers coming through can't teach and that is not the case. I've been in so many meetings where it is the first, second third year out teachers with the brilliantly fresh ideas. So I dislike the generalisation, but across the board there is a difference. We've got 22, 23 year olds coming out, that are teaching 17 year olds. A 70 year old who is teaching now, and they are some of the greatest teachers of all time, so I'm not being ageist ...They were going to high school in the early sixties. Education was totally different then, and you learn so much about how to teach, from the way you were taught. And the teachers who are coming out now, they were going to high school in the two thousand and tens. That's important.

Can a person be taught how to teach or do they need to be naturally suited to the role?

It's a bit of both. I'm going to sit on the fence. I've seen naturally brilliant teachers and you know they are a teacher the minute you meet them. There are students here, and I've even seen primary school kids, who are natural teachers. But they need to learn their subject areas. They still need to learn and fill their pedagogical toolkit. The flipside to that is I've seen people who are very subject orientated, with personalities not suited to teaching, but they have taught themselves to become brilliant teachers. So I think, yes, you can be taught to teach. I've seen it. Some people's disposition is more naturally suited to teaching but there is so much more to teaching.

<u>Given the huge impact of technology on teaching, where do you see the future of education?</u>

I think we have a tendency to speculate too far and to conclude that teachers will be redundant. Teachers will never be redundant, but the job will change.

It has always changed. It has changed in my time in teaching. AI is changing the game already. It's here. It is a bit like the internet. WE have to embrace it. We had to embrace the internet. We had to embrace word processing. Teaching will change and it will adapt. You are always going to need a teacher standing in front of the class. I think the teacher's role is already changing. Now, you are a counsellor, a motivator, sometimes you are a cook. You are a well-being coach. That's changed so much and it will continue to change. I remember hearing in my first five ten years of teaching, 'Why do we need to teach these young people how to be a good person? That should be happening in their homes.' You don't hear that anymore. I guess there is a different understanding of what a teacher is. That will continue to evolve. I can't speculate on what that evolution will be. Eighteen months ago I had no idea what AI was. I don't know what is out there so I don't know what the impact is going to be. But I do know we have to embrace technology because the jobs that our young people will have in twenty years' time, have not even been created. You can look at it two ways. You can say 'oh this is totally overwhelming. What do I do?' Or, you can embrace it as it comes. And I think as educators we need to embrace these new technologies and keep the fundamentals of what being a teacher is.

Look at mobile phones. We have a policy across all of our schools that there are to be no mobile phones in schools. I agree that mobile phones are the greatest disruption to classroom teaching. No doubt. But is putting a blanket ban on them in schools the best way to go about it? I think we need to explicitly teach young people on the use. The mobile phone is here to stay. How will they be in workplace? You aren't going to ban the mobile phone. We have to explicitly teach them the expectation around their use. That's bloody hard.

We all have awful days in education. But there is no other job I would rather do. I've seen young people grow into adults and become really valuable members of society. At times we need to stop and remember why we are in this job.

Afterword

Teaching has been a fantastic career for me. I came to it late and wished I had started earlier. I have made lifelong friends, been on trips overseas with those friends, and have been privileged to be a part of the lives of many young people. When you hear people criticise young folk you need to remember that there are a lot of good teenagers. They are finding their way in the world and yes, they make mistakes. Don't we all?

Since beginning this book I have retired from teaching. I still fill in once a week just to help out and get some good pocket money. My time at Trafalgar High School has been great. It went too fast, but it was such good fun. If you are thinking about a career in teaching I would advise you to give it a shot. It is not for everyone. Many people point out that they could not teach. They probably could. What they really mean is that they can't see themselves standing in front of 25 teenagers and interacting with them, let alone controlling them. Teenagers are people too. Give them a chance to surprise you and you will end up enjoying their company. A former colleague said two things about teaching; it keeps you young, and it is never boring.

Has it kept me young? Possibly. It certainly keeps the mind agile and you just have to have your wits about you to teach. And it definitely is not boring. Every day is different. Every week is different, and every year is different, which is odd in an institution that is grounded in set timetables, semesters and terms. The kids keep changing every year and the staff change a little bit every year as well. If you are new to teaching please remember that the time goes really quickly. At the end of every year you will stand around bidding farewell to a few members of staff.

I can recall thinking that the school just would not be the same when X leaves at the end of the year. But X left and the school trundled on. New staff arrived, and old staff retire or leave, until one day it is you standing in front of everyone giving a farewell speech.

I hope this book is not too negative. There are some wonderful things about our education system that the Department of Education and Learning has got right. There see? I can be positive. There are of course things that need to improve. But the people make it wonderful.

I am so glad I was a teacher.

About the Author

Stephen Higgins has been teaching for over twenty five years. He is a co editor of Aurealis, the Australian magazine of science fiction and fantasy. He co hosts the Apocryphal Australia podcast. He records instrumental music which is available wherever you get your music.